EVEN YOU CAN START A BUSINESS

EVEN YOU

CAN START A BUSINESS

From Startup to Success, a Step-by-Step Guide

CHRIS DALE

HOUNDSTOOTH
PRESS

EVEN YOU CAN START A BUSINESS

From Startup to Success, a Step-by-Step Guide

FIRST EDITION

ISBN   978-1-5445-3742-9 *Hardcover*
       978-1-5445-3740-5 *Paperback*
       978-1-5445-3741-2 *Ebook*

There is nothing special about me.

I definitely did not believe I had the ability to start and run a business.

I was just like you, the reader. This book is for you.

For the person who just wanted a little something for themselves.

For the person who wanted to make a difference
but not necessarily change the world.

For the person who had a dream of independence or
something more, no matter how small or insignificant.

For the person who wants to go on their own and does not know how.

This is for you.

CONTENTS

INTRODUCTION 9

PART I: BUSINESS BASICS

1. BEING A BUSINESS OWNER 23
2. WILL OWNING A BUSINESS MAKE YOU RICH? 27
3. SO WHERE DO I START? THE ESSENTIAL CHECKLIST 33
4. THE BUSINESS PLAN 43
5. TRUST YOUR GUT INSTINCT 53
6. DO YOU HAVE A MENTOR? 57
7. MIXING BUSINESS AND FAMILY 61
8. SHOULD I FUND IT ALL MYSELF OR DO IT WITH FINANCIAL HELP? 65
9. YOUR TARGET MARKET TRAP 71
10. ARE YOU GOING TO SELL A PRODUCT OR DO YOU OFFER A SERVICE? ... 77
11. DAVID VERSUS GOLIATH 85

PART II: THE BEGINNING

12. YOUR FIRST DAY 95
13. WHAT DOES THE END OF YOUR FIRST WEEK LOOK LIKE? 99
14. WHAT DOES YOUR ROLE AS CEO REALLY ENTAIL? 103
15. THE IMPORTANCE OF CUSTOMERS LOVING (*NOT JUST LIKING*) YOUR COMPANY ... 109
16. WHAT IS YOUR WORK-LIFE BALANCE LIKE IN THE EARLY YEARS? 113
17. IS DOING THE EASY THINGS ACTUALLY EASY? 121
18. WHAT ABOUT THE BIG WIN? 125

PART III: CULTURE

19. I HATE LOSING...AND THAT IS OKAY 131
20. IS THE DEAL EVER REALLY DEAD? 135

21. ARE YOU A MERCENARY OR A MISSIONARY?................................. 139

22. SHOULD YOU CHOOSE PRINCIPLES OVER THE MONEY?................... 143

23. TAKING ACCOUNTABILITY FOR EVERYTHING.............................. 149

24. WHY YOU SHOULD NEVER MAKE THE SAME MISTAKE TWICE........... 153

PART IV: KEEPING COSTS DOWN

25. OVERHEADS 159

26. WHAT IS YOUR BIGGEST WASTE OF MONEY IN THE MODERN ERA? ... 165

PART V: STAFF

27. BUILDING A TEAM 171

28. WORK ETHIC VERSUS TALENT... 175

29. DO YOU LIKE MANAGING PEOPLE? DO YOU REALLY WANT TO?......... 179

30. WHY DOES EVERYONE THINK THEIR EXCUSES ARE SPECIAL?
    IT IS YOUR JOB TO SPOT THEM 185

31. THE HIRING FAILURE CONUNDRUM... 189

32. THE GOLDEN RULES FOR LETTING A PERSON GO AT A SMALL BUSINESS 193

PART VI: A YEAR IN REVIEW

33. SO HOW DID I GET ON?.. 203

PART VII: THE MIDDLE

34. IF YOU ARE NOT ASSESSING, YOU ARE GUESSING 207

35. THE IMPORTANCE OF EXTERNAL RECOGNITION 209

36. THE NEXT STAGE AS A CEO.. 213

37. SALES 217

38. THE TEN-YEAR RELATIONSHIP... 221

39. LESSONS I HOPE YOU DO NOT HAVE TO LEARN THE HARD WAY 225

40. RELATIONSHIPS WIN DEALS—WHAT DOES THIS MEAN FOR YOUR BUSINESS? 231

41. BRINGING IT ALL TOGETHER 235

    ABOUT THE AUTHOR.. 241

INTRODUCTION

ARE YOU READY TO BE
YOUR OWN BOSS?

I always wanted to be my own boss but I never thought I was ready. If only I knew back then how hard and difficult setting up and running a business would be...I would have done it years ago.

Every book I have read about business, related to company success or management, is written by one of *the* most successful individuals or representing one of the largest companies on Earth. That makes sense; after all, these people have driven some of the most iconic and culture-changing companies and movements in recent times. However, every one I have read revolves around incredible speed of growth, with large external funding and 'seed rounds' (where the entrepreneur raises large amounts of money to fast-track their business through growth based on a future valuation or hoped valuation). Nine out of ten of these people are based in the affluent hills of Palo Alto,

California, and working in Silicon Valley in an incubator-style hub. Now, this felt so far from me and the 'real world that we live in' that it felt impossible. Then I realised what I wanted was not what they were describing. What I wanted was a little something for myself. Something smaller, but still successful, with the scope and opportunity for financial freedom and enjoyment.

Now, whilst these theories and lessons learnt are priceless and can be assigned to almost anyone trying to scale, they lack real-world application for 99 percent of people in the 'real world' who run companies with over ten or even fifty employees.

What about the person trying to do something on their own?

It actually overwhelms the honest individual hoping for a little something for themselves, wanting to take the leap. (Trust me, I know.) They especially do not represent the true small business leader just trying to find their way in the world. I have honestly never heard a person who operates a run-of-the-mill small business say, 'Wow, the way Mark Zuckerberg grew Facebook is something I am going to emulate' or 'How Larry Page fast-tracked Google is impressive. I think I will take a run at that'. (Although they are both super impressive achievements, may I add most people probably do not even know who Larry Page is!) I can find over a hundred stories about a person growing a company in California or New York to unicorn status (above $1 billion valuation)—trust me, I have the books.

What about success stories of a person from Slough (I will bet 99 percent of you outside of the UK have not heard of this place) or Sandusky, Ohio (picked for sentimental but obscure reasons), that went on to be a success in their own right? This made me question my definition of success itself. Perhaps I wanted something different—smaller, but special for me.

When I looked for guidance before I was starting out, it just did not exist—and boy, I wish it did!

There were no 'real-world' lessons.

There were no 'real-world' stories of pitfalls.

There was no real help. Full stop.

What I wanted to do was not glamorous, but that did not mean I did not need help.

Being a current small business owner and a nerd for personal growth books (or, as my mother calls them, self-help books), I have tried over the years to absorb many of the lessons I have learnt from these experts by standing on the shoulders of these giants and have tried to implement a portion of what is suggested into easily digestible scenarios that were relatable.

So why listen to me?

Because I am you. I am just an average person, from an average background. Because my plan is not to change the world. I want to create something for myself on a smaller scale, and that is okay.

But can I help other people like me that have an idea, a passion, and a dream for something more? I believe so.

This is important.

I am merely just another person setting up another company to try and achieve something for myself. I do not expect the *New York Times* to write about me or *Forbes* to interview me. Before I even set off on my business venture, I kept a log of my journey. The ins and outs of the day-to-day rises and falls. Although I probably represent the masses—810,316 small business were started in 2021—there is very little info about us.[1] We are actually the unsung heroes of the business economy, generating income, paying taxes, and providing jobs—perhaps not on a large scale individually, but as a collective, we are the largest contributor.

I do not pretend to be infallible, and I continue to make fundamental mistakes along the way, but what I can give you is a hands-on, warts-and-all understanding of what it takes to attempt to set up and run a small business, from day one up to the current day. It has been a rollercoaster of emotions, but you will get a truthful account of running a salt-of-the-earth, day-to-day business with honest, real-world (and occasionally ridiculous) problems and successes I came across. I will share how I celebrated the wins and crumbled under the losses. I will share with you the lessons I learned, and each one will end with a section on 'What I Wish I Had Known', meant to give you a head start in your journey.

I started from scratch with nothing more than an idea, determination, and hope for something more than what I currently

---

1   'Business Statistics', UK Parliament, December 21, 2021, https://commonslibrary.parliament.uk/research-briefings/sno6152/; UK SME Data, Statistics & Charts (2022)', Merchant Savvy, January 5, 2022, https://www.merchantsavvy.co.uk/uk-sme-data-stats-charts/.

had. But, like you, I did not know what I did not know. I had no idea how many challenges lay ahead in my journey to starting a business. Let us revisit the origins of my story so you can avoid the mistakes I made.

EVERYONE STARTS SOMEWHERE—THE HERO'S ORIGIN STORY

'Every Superhero has an origin story, telling how they gained their powers and decided to fight crime. It may be revealed in their first appearance, or not until an eventual flashback. But once established, it sets ground rules for which tropes are applicable to that particular superhero.

'The in-story explanation may be that the ultimate source of the hero's power is magic, Sufficiently Advanced Aliens, or Weird Science.'

—TV TROPES

First, I am definitely no hero. Just a regular guy who had aspirations for a little something of my own that I could share with similar great people.

A person who, deep down, had a nagging feeling that working for someone else just was not enough for him. A person who thought that his customer deserved better. Whose personal relationships he was struggling to maintain with his current employment due to the setup of his employers—nothing original here. Have you ever felt that way?

But the protagonist in every superhero story ever told has that breaking point. That moment of enlightenment or the inner battle that drives them to take a leap of faith in the name of all things good in the world. And in December 2017, that was my time!

When setting up a company, you deliberate for a seemingly infinite amount of hours, weighing up whether it is the right decision. You spend literal weeks considering if you are the right person to do this. Whether you even have the backbone or stomach for it (I will let you pick your body analogy).

Then you start considering the business side of things. Is there a gap in the market for what you are offering? How much money will it take to get the business off the ground? What should you call your company? What is going to be your unique selling point? How will your website look? These wonderful considerations are like a splinter in your mind that you cannot shift, but at the same time they fuel your creative flow over a period of months until you reach the conclusion that you are up to the challenge! You start piecing it together cohesively and constructively over a number of months, ready for a launch on your terms and time frames, organised and beyond excited to bring your offering to the world.

Yeah, that did not happen to me...

Token superhero movie flashback, five months earlier:

Mid-July, I handed in my notice at my former company—a behemoth of a company (four-hundred-plus employees at its peak) and market leading (by number of employees and turnover). I was fortunate to be in the upper echelons of the business, earning fantastic money in exchange for my soul and my moral compass. The company had not always been like that, but it is amazing what two rounds of private equity (which I did not benefit from, by the way) will do to dilute your ability to find the grey area in every black-and-white scenario and invite you to turn a blind eye.

After eleven years, I had reached my limit.

I had no issue with the eighty-hour working weeks when necessary, checking emails on family holidays, taking phone calls on national holidays (even speaking to a particularly enthusiastic Nigerian gentleman on Christmas morning), not being allowed to take more than a week's holiday at a time, or the eighty-five-plus overseas trips to Southeast Asia in economy class over seven years.

But what I had lost was the belief that the company was going to get better. I have always been competitive and hated not being the best at what I did, and in my current situation I saw no chance of short- or long-term improvement. I had spent the past four years slowly but increasingly papering over the cracks, lying to my team about the position of the company and trying to mend or maintain all my relationships in the market. The proverbial straw that broke the camel's back was in April that year, when one of my smallest customers, who had actually become a friend over time, pulled me aside and gave me a father-like talk, similar to the 'I am not angry; I am just disappointed' line every child dreads. He told me we would always be friends, but it was reaching a point from a business position where he just could not work with me anymore.

From this point, I explained to my boss that I had nothing

left, and we hatched a grand plan to set up together. (He was obviously feeling the same issues, as he was a rung higher up the ladder of corporate helldom.)

This sounds positive, does it not? Like a solid grounding for a new business. It was not.

The short version goes something like this:

- I was signed off with six months' gardening leave—win.
- I would have time to plan and make our offering the best in the market—win.
- I would launch with a cohesive plan, budgeting for success and growth, with a controlled and steady trajectory—win.

What actually happened instead:

- Delays—nothing got done on his part.
- Broken promises—he did not leave the company at all, like he had promised.
- Gaslighting—he stopped returning my calls and emails.
- Manipulation—he pushed blame and timings onto me.
- Control—he tried to get me to come back to the company I had just left, at a lower position.

Five months came and went with no signs of a new company.

At this point my gut was telling me something was not right. Having only two pay cheques left with nothing of any significance set up, I was beginning to panic. Although still excited (deep, *deep* down), I was not really sleeping, and I was almost praying that my partner would come good. My wife then pulled me aside and asked me the question that haunts anyone out of work who has jumped all in on a dream.

What is plan B?

To add to this, my business partner had just stopped returning my calls at all. Text messages were like gold dust too, mainly saying he was sorry; he was just so busy at work. Checking in just enough to keep me on the hook.

So what was plan B?

At that point, there was not one. Simple as that!

To make a long story short, my partner flaked out on me. After we spoke one day at his house, I finally realised the dream I had was dead as I hit rock bottom. The leap I had taken was wasted, and truthfully, I was screwed on so many levels I could not even calculate them all!

Going home that night, I was in full crisis mode. My wife was as supportive as they get (as she always is). Not a single 'I told you so'. He had pretty much stripped all my belief that I could do anything on my own. His final insult was the suggestion for me to head back to my old company in a lower role, knowing I was a failure without him. I still believe, to this day, he expected me to do exactly this.

This brings me back to the topic of this lesson. What driver does it take to set up a company? How about unbridled fear!

This fear spread across all different forms. The obvious fear came from within. First, how do I support my family now? Have I just wasted eleven years to start over again? But more importantly, how do I pay my mortgage without going on the beg to family? How do I pay my other bills?

I had one pay cheque due to me in a week's time. I had been living my life as a person (rightly) earning fantastic money each year. I had just gotten a massive mortgage a year earlier. I had the cliché 4x4 allroad vehicle on the drive and, most importantly, had two children and a wife to support.

Then it was more spiritual.

Was I good enough?

Did I want it enough?

Did I believe in myself enough?

Did I believe for one minute anyone would follow me?

Then it spread into the practicalities of it all.

How the hell do you set up a company? I have only ever done the front end of a company. I literally know nothing about the logistics, warehousing, pay or staff of a company.

How much money did I need to set up a company? Who on God's green earth was going to commit money to me with not so much as a company name?

Nothing kicks you up the arse to provide for your family more than fear and pride and a desire to be a success, or the idea of being a complete failure to the people who love you and rely on you! This gave me five weeks, or thirty-five days, or 840 hours (trust me, I counted) to get this company off the ground...

Challenge accepted.

Since then, I am over five years in, turning over £7 million in revenue and have twenty-seven staff. We are the market leaders in one of our two main fields and still growing. We have won multiple awards.

This book serves as the companion I did not have. I sincerely hope you are able to take these lessons to heart and avoid the mistakes I reveal in these pages.

PART I
BUSINESS BASICS

I wonder how many people have an idea for a business but never move forward with it?

I wonder how many people would take the leap if they just had more support at this early stage? I wonder how many people are gripped by fear of the unknown and how large the task at hand appears?

In the first part of this book, I aim to break down the pitfalls and experiences I came across before I launched my business.

I will cover how I got there, along with these other discussion points:

- How you can take this mammoth task and work through it, stage by stage.
- The problems I had to solve (which you may have to solve) and the physical and mental battles I had to face (which you may have to face).
- How the lessons I learnt were not always the most obvious and how my hindsight is a wonderful thing for your progress.

Following the next set of lessons will save you untold time and anguish, knowing that we have all faced the conundrums you are facing. If you just take one step at a time, you will be closer than you have ever been to something spectacular of your own.

BEING A BUSINESS OWNER

DO NOT BELIEVE THE HYPE!

The biggest lie ever sold about being an entrepreneur or owning/ running a business is that glamorous sports car / work-life balance / lunches / yachts image. Do you know the one?

You can visualise it, can you not? The one where they are driving with the top down in a Porsche or, better yet, chatting outside a café in Mayfair or the South of France whilst the business is running itself and making them money and they are living the life everyone dreams of.

Yeah, that is all a lie. A *complete* lie. Even if you did see it on Instagram. I want to clear that up right now. If that is your hope or belief, I would suggest you put the book down now.

First, no business, let alone one that you run and keep afloat, runs itself without your full and undivided attention. It just does not happen. And if it does happen, it does not happen for too long, and the money soon runs out.

Do not believe the myth!

So what is the truth? Here is my checklist:

- Sleepless nights? ✓
- Losing contact with friends? ✓
- Waking up in a cold sweat in the middle of the night because you do not think you are good enough? ✓
- Living without any real amount of disposable income in the first few years? ✓ Not a chance.
- Feeling more alone and cut off than anytime in your life? ✓ Absolutely.
- Having numerous occasions when you wish you had not taken this on, as it is not what you expected, and wish you just collected a salary and worked for someone else? ✓ Every damn month for the first three years! (Even in the successful months!)
- Being constantly mentally, physically and emotionally exhausted? ✓
- Realising that having any amount of staff is just a pain in the arse? ✓ More than ever.
- Having to tell yourself every damn day just to keep pushing, just keep persevering, that it is going to be okay, that it is going to be a success, with unwavering resolve, even if you do not really believe it? ✓ Too many times to admit.
- Dragging yourself out of bed when you have hit the tenth random obstacle that you did not expect that month? ✓ Every. Single. Month. (Seriously.)

Almost all owners and entrepreneurs have experienced these things, and you will too. But that is not the story they want to show. Who wants to be seen like that? They want the myth to follow them.

How many stories have you read about Steve Jobs as the most emphatic and inspirational entrepreneur of all time? I know that before I started my company, I thought he was a god. But even he had a side far less flattering than you would believe. You just do not hear it, as he was beyond successful as a businessman and the myth of Steve Jobs far outlives the real man.

The fallible human side that makes mistakes and cannot cope is in almost all cases the real-world version. But what they do show, which is accurate, is the sheer effort that went into establishing their businesses. You see the eighteen-hour days, and they are made into a badge of honour, like you have to do this to be successful. You have seen *The Social Network*, where Mark Zuckerberg cares more about creating Facebook than partying.

How glamorous was that in the film's portrayal?

What is not shown is the nervous breakdowns and fear of failure. The second-guessing of their ideas and their belief in what they were doing. The negative feedback from first clients or the many failed launches before the successful one.

No one ever shows the true version of a real-life trier. All we see are 'unicorns'. Trust me, there is a good chance you are not a unicorn that sleeps three days a month, shits gold and has clients queueing up to work with you at any price. I know I am not! All the ticked emotions and reactions above happened to me, and I love what I do!

I am an avid reader and love finding out what makes people tick. Even before setting up my business, I craved going into battle against the fear and making a success of whatever I put my mind to. I promise, in every single book you read, there is no reference or example that can truly convey just how difficult it is or how dark the hard times will be.

This is in no way aimed to scare you from doing something amazing. I just wish I had known and had someone who had been through it (even living vicariously through a book) to know it was not just me.

So when those moments come, know that they are natural and they happen to every single business owner on many occasions.

WHAT I WISH I HAD KNOWN

→ It is fucking tough! Possibly one of the toughest things you will ever do. But it is worth it.

→ Even the most wonderful business leaders of the ages would have gone through all the emotions listed above.

→ It is how you deal with the adversity that makes you who you are.

WILL OWNING A BUSINESS MAKE YOU RICH?

Money is definitely not the reason to set up a company. If you go in aiming to get rich quick, chances are you will fail.

However, to deny that at some point the money does matter is naive; you are only kidding yourself, and deep down you know it is a lie. Unless you are doing charity work somewhere around the world or trying to make a difference for humanity, money, at some point, is a driver for you. It should not be *the* driver, but everyone wants a better, more comfortable life. Understanding the numbers helps you appreciate the journey rather than the destination and manage expectations.

So what is the difference between £60,000 and £120,000?

You would be surprised to know that the difference between the two amounts of money is not so different.

Breaking it down by the numbers:

In 2021, the average salary in the UK was £31,285, according to national statistics.[2]

So £60,000 to £80,000 per year is a respectable salary that can help provide everything you and a family could need for a fulfilling life:

- Rent or a mortgage on a suitable property
- One family holiday a year
- A usable car or two
- Enough to pay your bills
- A perfectly comfortable way of life (outside of London)

But people (especially entrepreneurs like yourself) are constantly striving for the next stage and the next achievement level.

So what is the next level?

- Shopping at Waitrose versus shopping at Tesco or Asda?
- A holiday a year to the Caribbean versus a holiday to Spain or Portugal?
- An Audi versus a Ford?
- A four-bed house versus a three-bed house or two-bed apartment?

This is it. Not a huge difference, is it? Are you surprised?

---

2   'Average Annual Earnings for Full-Time Employees in the UK 1999–2021', Statista, November 15, 2021, https://www.statista.com/statistics/1002964/average-full-time-annual-earnings-in-the-uk/.

Let us look at an official breakdown of the numbers *after* tax, based on the UK calculation.

Gross salary: £60,000 versus £120,000.

Net salary after tax and national insurance: £43,489.16 versus £74,289.16.

The difference each month is *only* £2,566. A lovely bump, but would you call it life-changing?

Now add an extra £200 per month for shopping—that is Waitrose for you! Only the best from now on.

Add an extra holiday's cost, spread over a year—£250 per month—the Caribbean is not cheap! They are called the best beaches in the world for a reason.

A bigger/better car payment—£300—you cannot put a price on German engineering.

A larger mortgage—£800 per month—that extra bedroom for guests when they come to stay.

This totals £1,550 a month.

It soon adds up and then immediately gets eaten up. Once you understand the difference, it gives you clarity of thought on the reality of what you are undertaking and whether you want all the hassle of carrying a business on your back.

All that work for just under £1,000 a month more?

Now, I am not in any way telling you that the extra amount is not worth it. This is just to highlight in advance: What is important to you?

The forty-hour per week job pays £60,000 a year:

- You get your weekends and most evenings back.
- You can switch off your laptop and not take your work home with you.
- You do not have to worry about other people's salaries or payroll or admin or HR or logistics or suppliers.

The sixty- to seventy-hour week (especially at the beginning) that might pay £120,000 a year:

- You are open to calls and emails anytime you are not asleep.
- You worry about paying everyone, not just collecting a salary.
- You work on holidays.
- You never switch off.
- There is always a problem that needs solving.

In my opinion, was it worth it? One hundred percent. One of the best decisions of my life, regardless of the money. But is it right for you?

I took a 75 percent pay cut from my previous job in year one. I took a 50 percent pay cut in year two.

The first three months of setting up the company, my mortgage cost alone was higher than my net income. That is before bills, food, car, insurance(s), and all other payments. At the end of the first six months, my credit card was £300 away from being maxed out at £22,000.

So again, was it worth it? Even without looking back with rose-tinted glasses, as it has worked out, in those months my wife and I were in complete agreement that it was still better than the alternative.

By the way, I still earn 10 to 15 percent less a year than I did in my previous job. But the satisfaction and reward are one hundred times higher.

WHAT I WISH I HAD KNOWN

→ If money is the driver, prepare to be disappointed. Especially at the start.

→ It is very hard to stay disciplined with money as your salary increases. Your costs naturally go up.

→ In terms of a pounds per hour rate, working in a startup is not cost-efficient. You do not get paid for the 'extra hours'. They are built on goodwill forever.

SO WHERE DO I START? THE ESSENTIAL CHECKLIST

Carrying on the hero's origin story, once you know where you stand, either negatively or positively, it is liberating as you gain back control. My body literally shut down that night. It was a release of epic proportions. (This was the last time I slept like this for the next five years, may I add.)

I knew I had purpose. The next day was the start of something different. Who knew that letting go of all the 'what ifs' and changing my mindset could result in eight solid hours of sleep?

The next morning, I was on a mission!

I was humble enough to realise that I probably did not have a clue what I was really doing (this is okay, by the way), I was going to make a bucket load of mistakes, and I probably did not have the necessary talent in most areas. But what I did have was effort. I also had no backup plan and no desire to take a backward step and work for someone else again.

I have always believed that effort trumps talent (see Lesson 28). I have always believed if I could not be the smartest person, I would be the one putting in the most effort. I was going to live by this principle.

'Make sure you're the hardest-working person in the room.'

—THE ROCK

Getting a company off the ground sounds like a daunting task, when actually, it is an...outrageously daunting task! Who am I kidding?!

But like anything, it starts with one step, or in this case, one task, at a time. I always say to my son, 'Lionel Messi did not just become the greatest footballer. It started by kicking a ball'. And here I was. Right at the beginning. Learning to kick a ball.

IT ALL STARTS WITH A CHECKLIST—NO MORE, NO LESS

The wonders of the internet mean you can pretty much find out anything you need. It is not all useful—damn, it is not all true either—but if you can filter the rubbish, it can give you a guide and set you on a path.

You do not need an app to manage your time.

You do not need to voice-record messages to yourself.

You do not need spiritual reaffirmations.

You do not need anything that is going to distract you from the fear you are feeling or the anxiety you are dealing with.

All you need is an A4 piece of paper and a pen.

I broke my checklist down into the main key areas I believed I needed for my business (trust me, the subcategories were extensive), but one question was standing out more than anything else:

What do you honestly need to start a company?

You would think that there are a thousand separate things to do to get yourself off the ground. Google actually agreed with my thinking (fifteen billion answers, in fact!), *and I went down a rabbit hole of epic proportions.* But once you filter out the noise, below is a list of what is *really* necessary. Each point is then discussed in further detail.

1. A company name—this is as obvious as it sounds. You need one. A name that says exactly what you do. That is it.
2. A bank account—an account to receive and transfer money efficiently
3. A premise—to be discussed later, but most people need a version of a base
4. A product or service—in most businesses, I would assume you know who your basic suppliers are, what you are choosing to sell, or the service you are offering. It is a matter of a phone call to work with people. People want to do business. Do not overthink it.
5. A rough idea of clients to do business with—if you have not considered this before reading this book, shut it now. It is

not going to work. I am not expecting you to know who your specific clients will be or what your exact demographic is, but saying 'people on the internet' is a recipe for a long slog and a failed business.

Now let us examine each item in detail:

1. THE COMPANY NAME—IT IS NOT AS IMPORTANT AS YOU THINK

I stand by my original statement. The company name generally means nothing (or very little). If you are great at what you do, people will use you. Does it help when your company name tells, in some form, what you do? Sure. Is it a necessity? Absolutely not.

Nike, the leading sportswear brand in the world and a market icon and superpower for brand leadership, started as Blue Ribbon Sports and changed its name to Nike fourteen years later, in 1978. Do you actually know what Nike means? I did not until I looked it up for the book. It is the name of the Greek goddess of victory.

Who knew?! Now that you know, it is an awesome name in hindsight, but how many fifteen to twenty-four-year-olds do you believe know this? How many do you think care as long as their Air Force 1s are on trend?

Then take Google.

The company is iconic! It has had such an impact on society that it is now a verb in the English dictionary and controls a monopoly in search across the globe. However, I bet if you asked 99 percent of the population where the name came from, ironically, they would have to Google it.

It comes from the word *googol*. Meaning one plus one hundred zeroes. Who knew? And who honestly cares? If I said, 'What does Tesla do?' would you associate it with electric cars before you knew what they did? Or how many people would know *peloton* was a word linked to surrounding a key rider in cycling so they perform better as a group?

You get the point. Actually, once a lot of companies get to a size where a large proportion of the world knows what they do, they shorten their name, as it is just synonymous by that stage with what they do. Even in the beginning, Apple was Apple Computers, and if Apple believes you need to know what they did at the start, then trust me, so do you.

For small businesses, it does make it easier sometimes to slap someone in the face with what you do. Calling yourself John Smith Audio, for instance, sounds pretty obvious, but it is still actually very general. What sort of audio do you do? Cars? In home? Events? How will the person know to find what they are looking for?

John Smith BMW Car Audio does exactly what it says on the tin. Small businesses are all about being niche, so do not make it harder than it needs to be. You are going to appreciate every possible customer when the time comes—make it as easy as possible for them to find you and not ask as many questions to make a decision.

The point is to come up with a few names. Pick the best one.

Check to see if it is available as a web address. Buy it. Commit to it. Done. On to the next thing. There are bigger issues to solve coming up; trust me!

2. A BANK ACCOUNT

Online business banking is easily accessible. Or you may just need a personal account, which you may already have, to start off.[3] Yes, there are business banking offers and bonuses for signing up, but right now, in this moment, you need the ability to purchase goods and services and receive funds for orders. Nothing more, nothing less. It takes ten minutes online. Get it done and move on.

3. PREMISES

With the way technology has advanced, how many of you truly need actual premises when starting up? There is also a difference between premises to accommodate staff and premises to hold stock. If you do not need them for stock, then this is a phase two or three problem. Do not make the mistake of this outlay early on. I discuss the huge waste of money it can be in Lesson 25.

However, if you are a business that holds inventory to sell, it can be a necessity, so it stays on the list. Just be careful, and lean into it gently. Test the water with how much space you need, ideal location and so on. You can ramp this up temporarily really easily, but it is much harder to reduce once you have committed to something more permanent.

---

3   This is only applicable if you are a sole trader, as the government treats your personal income and business income as one for tax purposes.

When I set up, we went from a generic, small monthly rental storage lock-up for four months, to a bigger version for the following three months, to a small warehouse for four years, to our current premises, which are double the size (which actually crossed over for a year, due to need). Depending on the size of your company and the product you sell, your own living room can serve as useful for the first few months to keep costs down.

4. A PRODUCT OR SERVICE YOU INTEND TO SELL

I would strongly recommend that you have an idea of what you want to offer the world before taking the leap. You do not have to know the minute details, but if you decide that you are going to first quit your job and then come up with an idea for a business, I would strongly dissuade you from doing it. It is one of the few times you are probably not ready, and the risk is too high.

For a large percentage of people reading this book, you will know the industry you want to work in. You will also have an idea of the product you want to sell. It is then a matter of a phone call to work with that supplier and buy stock.

5. CLIENTS TO DO BUSINESS WITH

As per number four, if you have not considered this before reading this book, please shut it now. It is not going to work. Again, be more specific than saying 'people on the internet'. Most people starting their own small business have experience in that field before doing it for themselves. They will also have clients they hope will follow them into their new venture.

What you do not need:

A logo or a slogan—unless you are creating a clothing brand or the newest, coolest alcoholic beverage. A logo is a bonus. Your name is your logo. Who needs a snappy catchphrase these days, really?

'*A logo is a symbol made up of text and images that identifies a business. A good logo shows what a company does and what the brand values. Logo design is all about creating the perfect visual brand mark for a company.*'

—99DESIGNS

Pick a font you like for your company name. That is now your logo. Every company has changed their logo as the company and times have evolved, and these are multibillion-dollar monsters. Just google Pepsi's logo evolution for a great example.

This should take no more than five minutes. Another task off your list.

At this stage you barely know who you are as a person, let alone your company's brand values.

A team—day one is you against the world. Anything more is probably a distraction and too far ahead of what is needed.

However, some people do have a grand vision. Having an idea of who you are going to build your business with is amazing. In fact, any person who has considered creating something, no matter how small, will have considered employees, even if it is just one or two. But unless that person does something you physically cannot do or cannot learn, it is not for day one. I knew I could not do, and had zero knowledge of, warehousing (which was needed for the service we provided) or the providers of inventory, so my business partner was the yin to my yang. However, ideally, you need to have a company on day one that you and you alone could run if you had to.

I still knew this deep down; I just *really* did not want the aggravation.

For 90 percent of people reading this, business will be stepping into unknown territory. Get the basics sorted, *then* assess who you need.

Bonus: do not be afraid to ask for help.

We all have our strengths. Where people go wrong is believing they are best to solve all problems that need solving. Then it is having too much pride to ask for help. As you can probably tell, after everything that had happened, I was way past that stage. I called in any favour I possibly could.

After the business partner fiasco scenario in my origin story, I am not ashamed to say I called in a favour from my mother (she is super savvy) to set up the stuff on Companies House (the official registry for companies in the UK). I called a friend to help with reserving the necessary web addresses. (I had done the research on names.) I begged another friend to build out a basic website. I contacted a temporary storage facility to inquire about costs of space. Even my wedding invite designer was called upon (see another niche successful business) to start work on a draft business card and 'brochure'—*I felt I needed this to be reputable. I did not. Waste of money. But lesson learnt.*

WHAT I WISH I HAD KNOWN

→ You are never fully ready. You just need to be ready enough.

→ Grit, determination, belief, pride, fear or proving a point can be amazing drivers. Use your inner power to your advantage.

→ You can only plan so much. Never does everything go completely right.

→ Do not overthink things. Work with structure and efficiency.

→ Make sure your company name is as obvious as possible to explain what you do.

→ Make sure your company name is available online—do not register the name on Companies House and then try and get the web address. Work the other way.

→ There is nothing on the checklist that cannot be changed later. But you need to start somewhere.

THE BUSINESS PLAN

'Plans are worthless, but planning is everything.'

—SCOTT GALLOWAY

Before you go any further, before you come up with a name, the business plan (although less enjoyable) is the most important stage one process you have to undertake. This is the crash to reality of whether you have a viable business opportunity.

If you have the funds to bankroll your enterprise, your business plan does not need to be as detailed—after all, if it all goes wrong, it is your money you are losing. However, if you intend to be taken seriously and pitch for a form of financial backing, no matter how informal, the more detail you can give, the lower the chances of being rejected.

People naturally stress about this, obviously, because this is the first time, outside of the friends and family you have 'pitched' your idea to, that real-life people are going to judge you. I know for a fact I could have pitched my mum and wife as some sort of drug-dealing pimp and they would have still seen the positives and told me it had potential.

I want to make two main points regarding the business plan:

1. KNOW YOUR SHIT

If you go and pitch for funding and you do not know your business inside out, and they quiz you on the basics and you cannot answer, then grab your coat because the pitch is over and you have wasted everyone's time.

Think *Dragons' Den.*

Ever watched those people who cannot answer simple questions about their business in front of the experts? They do not deserve other people's money. If you do not know your business, you do not deserve to get the funding, and it serves you right if this happens to you.

Talk about learning a life lesson.

It ends up being a waste of your time and theirs. Have you ever gone into a shop to buy a TV or a phone and spoken with a salesperson who did not know what they were talking about when you asked for their advice? How likely are you to hand over a substantial amount of money to that person and buy that item? Probably not very. It is no different here. You are the salesperson.

Do not know what you intend to sell a product for? How can you possibly calculate gross margin? How can you possibly forecast costs and profit? How are you going to sell it?

Do not know who your target market is? Who are you going to call on day one? The point is, you have a duty to know your business.

2. UNDER-PROMISE AND OVER-DELIVER

Whenever I have put a business plan together, I have always tried to put down worst-case scenarios. This is for two reasons.

First, I am a salesperson at heart and it is *always* better to under-promise and over-deliver—*always*! This offers many advantages, both short- and long-term, to the person you are selling or pitching to.

Subconsciously and without knowing it, the person receiving the information is always going to be happy that the results are better. Imagine you are on Tinder and you see a profile and find them attractive. You look at his bio and it says he is six feet two with an athletic build (or the female equivalent). You build a picture in your mind of what you expect. Then when you get there, if that person is five feet nine and overweight, your natural reaction is to be disappointed. (For the record, this happened to me with a woman when I was very young, so I have firsthand experience.) This is an extremely shallow example, but it highlights the point. If that person had been honest, they would have had a better chance of a successful date.

Now imagine, from a business point of view, that you sell a customer a TV. You tell them they can have their product delivered in seven days. It is in stock and, above all else, you offer a full installation service as part of the deal. But the truth is you are booked up for the next two weeks, it is out of stock, you will need to supply a suitable replacement and the promise of full installation service really means just standing it on the media unit and taking away the rubbish—not actually hanging it on the wall or programming it.

Do you think that customer would give you a five-star review and use you again? No.

Even though it was a manageable situation you were in at the start, the eagerness to please actually ruins the experience. Now I have spent my life saying it will be a longer delivery time than it is. If it is not in stock, we will *upgrade* you, free of charge, and make sure the 'setup' is more comprehensive than expected. (No, I do not sell TVs.)

So when we deliver in a shorter amount of time, swapping out the item for something 'better' and fully fitting the new product, the client thinks we are the best thing since Netflix. Same offering, rephrased.

Second, you are kidding yourself if you think putting forward punchy sales numbers and low costs to make yourself look better or more profitable is wise. You are creating pressure on yourself to deliver at the maximum level with zero wiggle room or allowance for outside influence. Trust me, there is always something you have not accounted for.

In all areas of business and life, under-promising and over-delivering has its merits. When you are creating a business plan, you do not know many hidden costs associated with running a business. I know I did not. On paper, my business plan had conservative sales numbers against high costs to minimise expectations.

We have smashed sales numbers every year so far. But, wow, did I learn a hard lesson on costs and expenditures that I could not have come close to fathoming before I started. In year three, I had sales of £4 million budgeted and profits of £800,000 against that, after costs. To say I was not close is an understatement. It was laughable. I exceeded and did £4.6 million in sales, but the profit calculation was nowhere near!

Below, I share my original business plan with you as an example to help illustrate the things I wish I had known.

MY BUSINESS PLAN

Even under my personal circumstances (fear and time restraints), I took the time to write down exactly what I wanted from my company. This was to give clarity of thought (as, at the time, I was working from caffeine and adrenaline) but also to make sure if I was going to do this, I did it right. Everyone has a perfect scenario. That scenario gets watered down in your head, especially over time, and unless you come back to it, you forget what it originally looked like. I did not want this to happen to me. The previous company that had employed me had slowly run itself down from a really iconic brand in the industry to something I did not recognise chasing money.

To give context to this book, I believe it is best to be honest about what (in my mind) was my ideal scenario.

GOALS

Turnover: To *limit* sales to £5 million a year. (I use the word *limit* on purpose.)

Turnover is deceptive. For some people, a number as high as £5 million is a ridiculously large amount and does not seem like a small business at all. If you are selling toilet paper or marbles, you would be one of the largest specialist businesses in the country. If you are selling yachts, this amount accounts for about a tenth of one average boat and would just about cover a dinghy to get you to it.

For my business, £5 million was a healthy turnover, in my eyes, without me having to have the big warehouse with hundreds of staff and chase every order out there—as mentioned before, been there and done that, never again.

To give more context, the biggest company in our niche area of business turned over £40 million, with another at £20 million, a couple at £8 million to £10 million, and then a bunch scattered between £4 million and £6 million (according to Companies House). This target amount would allow me, in my eyes, to take on the big projects but still be niche and concentrate on a handful of great clients.

However, telling potential investors or shareholders that you want to cap your turnover is the opposite of everything you are ever told to do when pitching for money. Can you imagine saying that on *Dragons' Den* or *Shark Tank* when pitching to the investors? You would be laughed out of the building. However, that is what I did.

STAFF

In my head, twenty people was the dream number. If we had only the highest-quality employees, this would be the right amount of staff to take the total value of orders listed above, based on previous experience. We could manage the clients and deliver the finished product to the highest standards of customer service. In my industry, six of those twenty were installation staff, so we were only looking at fourteen inbound and outbound staff, including myself and my business partner.

As I had worked in the industry for eleven years at this point, I also had a strong idea of who the best people in it were. This helped craft a broad outline of a future plan for the next three/six/twelve months, should everything go well.

SALARY

We were to pay better than anywhere else. I am not talking Google and Facebook staff–level rewards, but for our marketplace, our goal was to hire the best. In return, we expected the best.

We wanted free thinkers, people who loved what they did, people who could interchange between roles at times, should areas need help. More importantly, they had to be the best at what they did. Our theory was if we got that right, we would get more hours from them and the results would be exponentially better than good staff. Quality over quantity.

CULTURE

The majority of people I potentially wanted to hire at the new company had, at different points, suffered the same experiences as I had. Over-promised and under-delivered on a yearly basis (the opposite of the last chapter's advice), average pay whilst being worked into the ground, deception around communication regarding the company and bonuses, bad holiday allowance, and lack of trust, no matter your length of service (you were never believed if you were ill, for instance). At the same time, I imagined (and now know, running a business), the more employees you have, the harder it is to be free flowing. Procedures are there for a reason. However, this was not going to be us.

LOCATION

Even in bricks-and-mortar-based businesses such as mine, which required holding huge amounts of stock, I had experienced firsthand that expensive locations were a mistake (see Lesson 25). Again, if staff are self-motivated, hard-working, and adaptable, 90 percent of them can work from almost anywhere. We were not to waste money on overheads. If you sell to an international clientele, having a domestic base becomes a bit ridiculous.

TARGET MARKET

The aim was always to have far fewer clients than before but offer a far more personalised, attentive service. To be not just a provider but an extension of their business. I knew this was not always going to be possible, but if we strived to achieve this with every customer we dealt with, it would hold us in good stead.

Rather than diversifying into lots of areas within our industry, as lots of our competitors had done to chase growth, we were to aim at two areas that were interlinked by location, demographic and basic service undertaking. We were going to be *the* specialists, no matter what.

Ironically, the one time I tried to diversify, due to the pandemic (going against my own rules), it went completely wrong, made virtually no money and spread us thin, and our core industries continued to boom over 30 percent in a year. Serves me right! Do not be like Chris!

FUNDING

I knew I wanted to fast-track the business. I knew there was a gap in the market and that doing it slowly had as many pitfalls as doing it fast. Being of a reasonable size potentially aided areas such as buying power, deliveries and client capture. *I was also super impatient to prove myself after my previous employment.*

WHAT I WISH I HAD KNOWN

→ Know who you want to be as a company. If you do not, take the time to think about it.

→ For a small business, niche is good. Do not cast your net too wide or you will not catch anything.

→ Do not underestimate culture. It will become one of your most important assets. It is the part I am most proud of.

→ Make sure you know your business. I mean, really know it. You should be the most knowledgeable person on your business at all times. It is yours, after all.

→ Your costs will be higher. They just will. Take that into consideration.

→ Try and be realistic about what you want to achieve—this will set the aims and tone for everything.

TRUST YOUR GUT INSTINCT

IS IT YOUR SECRET WEAPON?

This rule is right up there in the most important lessons of running a business that rarely get discussed. This rule is actually important in most areas of a person's life. I am not pretending it is a perfect tool, but it definitely has helped me when making tough decisions.

You can look at data and make decisions day-in, day-out with your head and be fine and function and grow your business. But you will come across moments in your business where that nagging feeling in your stomach is giving you the needed direction that does not make complete sense. The lesson I have learnt is if you go with your head and it is wrong, you can validate it as you over thought it or it was the logical thing to do. If you make a decision against your gut instinct and it is wrong, wow—it is tough to accept. My gut instinct is my compass on big decisions. I do not listen to it blindly, but deep down I know if my gut instinct believes it, then long-term, it will be right.

About six months into the company, we had a chance to pitch for a multi-deal project. We were already on a preferred supplier agreement list with the company, so we were one of two companies invited to tender. However, although the 'relationship' existed, deep down we knew it was not as strong as we hoped.

This was alarm bell number one.

Although we were one of two companies on the list, we were an obvious second. We got our business through secondary channels rather than direct from the client and had been used as an alternate quote to help close business for the other company on many previous occasions.

But it was for a huge deal, and it would have made our whole yearly sales target as a business. So, as you do, we dropped all other potential business and committed to make the tender as comprehensive as possible.

When the tender document was distributed to us, the second alarm bell was ringing especially loudly again. The document already had the competing company's name on it. Obviously, I had to inquire about the reason, and I was assured that originally the other company was put forward for the project, but it was important that the best company work on it and the client was now 'unsure' about the other company. At this point, I knew it was not ours to win. But still I persevered and agreed that to win this tender, our presentation would have to be worlds apart from the competition in quality. As this was what our company set out to do, we were going to blow them away!

The presentation date arrived. We pitched with bells and whistles. We blew them away. For every question they asked, we had a fully broken down, comprehensive answer for them. As we left, they told us how shocked and impressed they were with us as a company and with our presentation. They even told us we had given them ideas and raised inquiries that their team had not even come up with. It was a huge success!

And we lost it.

Why? Because the deal was not ours to win. The relationship was not there, and it would only have been ours to win if the other company had not metaphorically turned up. Sounds like an excuse, does it not? (Which I *hate*.) But you know when you know, you know. It was one of those moments.

My gut instinct told me this at the start. Why did I not listen? It told me again when I got the tender document. Why did I not listen then?

I knew we were going to lose it, yet I still persevered. I wasted so much time and energy, both my own and my team's, on a hapless endeavour. I cannot tell you how pissed off at myself I was afterwards, especially as I was not even shocked we lost it. I even said before the document came through, 'We are not going to win this'.

So why? In this instance, I think it was a mix of things. Greed— knowing the value of the project, I just could not walk away. Ego—wanting to prove my instinct was wrong (an internal battle) and wanting to be approved (everyone strives for this in different facets of their life, do they not?). I always say, 'You have to be in it to win it' and everyone has a 'puncher's chance', so surely you have to live by your mantras? Surely?

Second, deep down it was the competitive nature of sales and being determined to win the 'relationship' over and show them that I was better than what they had and they should like me more (see above about approval).

Either way, I was an idiot and wasted a bucketload of time, all because I did not listen to my gut instinct.

Do not do what I did. Do not *be like Chris.*

WHAT I WISH I HAD KNOWN

→ Your gut instinct is a tool in your toolbox. Listen to it.

→ As you grow, your gut instinct will become more refined to each and every situation.

→ Do not let ego and need take over. Short-term loss over long-term impact. Take the short-term loss every time.

DO YOU HAVE A MENTOR?

IF NOT, GET ONE

Everyone has a mentor. Anyone who says they have not had a mentor in their life is lying to you! Virtually every successful person in history has had some form of a mentor in life, business or family.

Steven Spielberg was a mentor to J. J. Abrams. Maya Angelou mentored Oprah Winfrey.

However, when you set up a new business, you lose sight of the need for a mentor. This could be because you can no longer look up to someone at work (as you are now the top dog) or because you are too busy or, even worse, do not think you need one. Do not make this mistake. This is the time you need one more than ever.

Mentors give you perspective; mentors ground you with their stories and advice and experience. Even if all this is not completely relatable, having a sounding board is very important. You are new to this. You cannot expect to make all the right decisions. Who is there to filter you?

As I have gotten older, my mentors have changed. First was my mum—the ultimate mentor and ball of positivity encouraging me that I could do anything. She literally told me to reach for the stars (that is actually one of her sayings) and that I could be anything.

I then had my work mentor, who nurtured me, taught me the lay of the land, protected me, and fast-tracked me to success. But, as mentioned previously, I eventually saw both sides and outgrew him.

Then, as I started my own business, I found that mentors in my life that I could relate to were hard to come by. I had a client of mine that was about eight years ahead of me in business. He was very successful, we had a lot in common and he was well-rounded with a family, but that was about it. I could always ask his advice, but our time spent together was limited due to work and family commitments.

This led me to examine what I needed from a mentor and where I could find it. As I could not find the physical person to fill that role, I actually turned to books and podcasts.

Nervous about your business growing too fast or too slow? There is a book for that. Worried you are not investing your money well? Let me introduce Warren Buffett and then go down a rabbit hole to a hundred other people. These experts are easy to find and help you develop.

I reckon I read two books on self-improvement in my first eleven years of work and I read eleven books in the first two years since setting up my business. Everything from positive psychology to business patterns, to working on my strengths, to the successes of specific businesses like Google. Each of them adding to the tools at my disposal as a business leader.

You need to make a conscious effort to find a mentor. I promise it will benefit you in the long run. If that does not work, it is time to dust off that Kindle!

WHAT I WISH I HAD KNOWN

→ A mentor is an impartial sounding board who can hedge your thoughts and ideas and who is not directly linked to the business.

→ Real-world experience is important (hence the book), even if not directly related to your industry. A lot of the lessons are transferable.

→ How can you expect to be an expert on all things? You have only just started.

MIXING BUSINESS AND FAMILY

A MATCH MADE IN HEAVEN OR HELL?

There is a myth. The myth says that especially at the start of a new business, getting family members to help out in your venture will benefit you. This is true in businesses with low margins or unsociable hours, as you can leverage your relationship to make it work for you for the 'common good'. This is prevalent in restaurants and family shops where you are all linked to the success of the business and success is predicated on a basis of hard work over skillset and ability. *Never forget this*, as this is where the pros of working with family members end.

Let me break down the problems from start to finish.

1. THE IDEA AND CONCEPTION STAGE

When discussing an idea with your parents or family members (minus perhaps your partner), what is it you are expecting to hear? Do you think you are going to get an honest, impartial discussion on the merits of the industry, with research and understanding, in a concise and structured way?

Of course not.

The reaction is going to be from their heart, not their head, nine times out of ten. They have a genetically vested interest to 'protect you' or help guide you. Would you ask a neurobiologist how to sell cars? Of course not. You get the point. So why would you bounce an idea for a business off a parent who has no knowledge of what the business and risk entail?

2. THE ALL-OR-NOTHING RESPONSE

You will either get the talk about risk or their full support to go for it. Test it. I bet you this will be the outcome.

As their feedback will be based on emotion, passion and love, their reaction will be extreme either way. Anyone who has even thought about setting up a company has had the lecture from a parent about how working for someone has its perks, such as security and pension and a steady pay cheque when you have bills to pay (protection). Your partner is different, as they have a duty to question this leap if you have family or financial responsibilities, regardless of how good the idea is.

The opposite of this is when, after a two-minute brief on the business, you get, 'Oh, that sounds amazing, you have to go for it...what have you got to lose?' Whilst this is lovely and supportive, you still do not know, other than your belief, whether it is a worthwhile venture. (I may add that your belief is more than enough, and this, I am sure, is one of the driving factors for people taking the leap. Belief can move mountains. But still, how constructive is the response?)

The issue here that I am trying to highlight is that pitching them an idea is a wasted venture to receive anything beneficial. In fact, it may muddy the water on your idea without any constructive feedback. There are better people to discuss this stage with.

In fact, almost anyone is better to discuss it with.

If you are just looking for reassurance that you are doing the right thing or looking for a way out due to cold feet, then these conversations are perfect, as you can frame them accordingly and get the desired response.

Otherwise, seek out someone not emotionally invested in you for sound reasoning and advice. Everyone knows a person. It will take guts to open up and pitch an idea knowing you will get true feedback.

WHAT I WISH I HAD KNOWN

→ Separating family from work, especially in the early stages, is crucial, except for anyone directly affected by it financially in the short term.

→ Find a suitable sounding board who will give feedback constructively, not emotionally.

→ Family has their place in your journey. This is not it.

SHOULD I FUND IT ALL MYSELF OR DO IT WITH FINANCIAL HELP?

Bootstrapping versus external funding. What are they and which one is right for me?

It is better to know at the beginning rather than during your journey, as how you frame everything moving forward is dictated by this decision. A lesson I wish I had known.

Excusing the investing lingo, there are two equally successful ways to start up a business.

BOOTSTRAPPING

In layman's terms, bootstrapping is building a company from the ground up with nothing but personal savings and, with luck, the cash coming in from the first sales. The term is also used as a noun:

'A bootstrap is a business (an entrepreneur) with little or no outside cash or other support launches.'

—INVESTOPEDIA

For most small business startups, this is seen as the only way to do it. The idea of borrowing other people's money or letting others have a stake in your newfound baby feels the furthest from what you would want to do.

And you know what? This is fine.

I was torn with what path to take when setting up. I had very limited time, even more limited money for mortgage payments, let alone funding the company, and above all, I was torn emotionally.

After all I had been through, the idea of giving up a slice of my company to an 'outsider' felt like I was being robbed or cheated. Plus, in my mind, I was obviously going to be a huge success (delusions of grandeur), and they were going to piggyback and make money off of me. For the record all of these were both fair and warped ideas at the same time.

When you ask people about this subject, you rarely get a valid and fair discussion. From people who have not done one or the other, you will get an extremely one-sided discussion on the merits of one over the other. So I have broken it down for you.

THE PROS OF BOOTSTRAPPING

You are completely accountable—you expected to do it all yourself anyway, so there is no difference there. I will live by the sword and die by the sword. It is my idea, and I have waited this long; anything less feels like I am diluting my dream.

No one can dictate to you the direction of your business—how dare they! This is mine and mine only. I know best, and any outsider will just be in it to make money. I believe in what I am doing for more than the financial rewards.

There are no expectations. You can control your pace and growth no matter how fast or slow. I do not need someone on my back chasing to get their money back.

THE CONS OF BOOTSTRAPPING

Everything will move at a slower pace. Money gives you choices. Buy more stock, hire more staff, acquire bigger premises. Just general growth opportunities.

A sounding board can offer constructive criticism and direction and also act like early customers (in my instance).

EXTERNAL FUNDING

'Investing is the act of allocating resources, usually money, with the expectation of generating an income or profit.'[4] You can invest in endeavours, such as using money to start a business, or in assets, such as purchasing real estate in hopes of reselling it later at a higher price.

---

4   Will Kenton, 'Understanding Profit', Investopedia, May 19, 2021, https://www.investopedia.com/terms/p/profit.asp.

THE PROS OF EXTERNAL FUNDING

No individual or business will hand over their hard-earned cash if they do not believe that there is going to be a return on their investment. They must believe in what I am doing or that there is a gap in the market; otherwise, why would they give me their money?

You will have the ability to react to market changes quickly—money gives you choices. Having the ability to react to potential deals by buying stock or labour could increase profits or help win new clients.

If you are worried about the risk involved, it can take the pressure off you if you have not put every last penny in—it would be good to know that I can afford to pay myself for a few months whilst this all gets up and running.

THE CONS OF EXTERNAL FUNDING

At some point, the investors are going to expect a return on their investment. I loved the accountability, but for others it is an unneeded distraction and pressure—I am on the clock. What if they start pressuring me for profits when I want to reinvest the money into the business to make it successful? What if I have a bad month or year?

You are giving away a slice of the business. I have waited so long to do this. Is this short-term investment going to benefit me long-term, or am I going to regret it?

When it came to this decision for me, it was an easy one once I had broken it down. I knew (believed), having worked in my industry, that there was a niche for my offering, so I wanted to fast-track it as much as possible. As mentioned previously, I was impatient and wanted to stick it to the powers that be. I also knew there were certain aspects I just could not do on my own (specialist areas in the back end), so I needed a few staff. I knew and still know my limits. My theory was that owning a piece of the business is only worth it to investors if the business is a success. Otherwise, they would own 17.5 percent of nothing. I saw it as all risk for them and all reward for me.

The other final point to consider is that I am not greedy. I was not in this for the short-term or the quick fix. I was too young to retire and genuinely believed I could create something amazing with a group of people I love. I was always taught that 100 percent of zero is zero. I may be a capitalist, but I was also a pragmatist and a bit of a dreamer.

WHAT I WISH I HAD KNOWN

→ No one choice on how you fund your business is right or wrong. Just make sure it is right for you.

→ If you go looking for investors, make sure you find the right ones.

→ Make sure you can handle the pressure of having other people's money.

YOUR TARGET MARKET TRAP

When you are first setting up a company and are looking for outside funding, fundamentally, people want to know the target market. It is good for you to have a gauge on it too.

'A *target market is a group of customers with shared demographics who have been identified as the most likely buyers of a company's product or service.'*

—INVESTOPEDIA

The natural reaction is to pool anyone and everyone into the field. If you take Google as an example, technically their target is for every person in the whole world to have access to search— roughly 7.6 billion people (as of 2021). Now, that sounds like a wonderful number and is a reason why they are worth close to $1 trillion.

But with a small business, this is the wrong way to look at it. You have limited resources within your team, so trying to target every person who could possibly give you business is a recipe for failure.

Peter Thiel (one of the founders of PayPal and the first investor in Facebook) says, 'it's easier to dominate a small market than a large one.'[5] Amazon, although known as 'The Everything Store' thanks to the Jeff Stone book of the same name, originally only sold books because there was 'a niche online to sell more books than any one bookstore could hold and sell.'[6]

Facebook originally created a community just for Harvard students to link up and communicate. Only once the uptake there had saturated did they link to another university. You get my point. Even if we are trying to offer a much smaller version of this, the principle applies.

In my case, when I first set up, I identified one particular client that I felt was ripe for disruption, that I could make the biggest difference to and that would see me as a star. There was no point in me going for the best in market at this stage. My offering was not perfect and had its faults. Also, when you try and impress people who are already at the forefront of what they do, eliciting a wow-factor response is so much harder, as the level of expectation is so much higher.

My target client was big by size (so had capacity to give enough business) but not hierarchically difficult to break into. (Lots of companies have loads of 'directors' that all have to approve, so you never get full buy-in initially. The bureaucracy makes

---

5   Peter Thiel, *Zero to One: Noes on Startups, or How to Build the Future* (Sydney: Currency, 2014).

6   Brad Stone, The Evverything Store: Jeff Bezos and the Age of Amazon (London: Bantam Press, 2013) [page number].

everything take so long.) They had a good, solid reputation in the marketplace—so it was good to be associated later down the line when using them as a reference. The staff were grounded individuals, so to speak. Normal people from normal backgrounds, so they were easier to relate to when pitching for business. (This is massively important, as people make judgments immediately whether you are one of 'their type of people'.) They were divisional, so we could divide and conquer, and our results were not linked to one big win or loss. Get it right (which we did), and then move more easily into other divisions by recommendation. I could offer them a variety of different services. My service worked because, normally, when one area was slow, the other picked up, due to the nature of the marketplace. So we had a steady stream of inquiries. Last, their current offering was average at best, so when we charged into each division, they were genuinely blown away!

When it all started, I had one contact there, which I would rate as a 5 or 6 out of 10 for strength of relationship. I had done some business before with them and been reliable and consistent, but the director himself was in the rarefied air and could not have cared less about what I really did as a contractor. His understudy I had met twice, and she openly says she thought I was an idiot the first time we had lunch. (She also did not use the word *idiot*!)

From the relationship with that one contact (who left after year three), that client now accounts for 15 to 20 percent of our annual turnover as a company.

If you take that company and break it down:

- One company
- Nineteen divisions
- Nineteen marketing directors
- Nineteen sales directors
- Approximately one hundred managers with influence

We literally started with one!

We networked the shit out of one person into another. Word of mouth x good job = more contacts.

Try, test and repeat.

Even now, we have just gotten in with our seventh division. We have also identified that probably ten divisions are not suitable for us or our product (due to price—we are too 'high end' for their lower-value areas). This leaves two still to go, six years in. Whereas before we relied on the biggest division for revenue, now our order book is spread across the areas, so the total revenue is up, but the reliance on one or two divisions is diluted. If these divisions have a quiet year, we are not scrabbling around for new business.

For any small business startup, if you can find one client that you can develop, expand and maximise the return of, concentrate on this. Chasing constant new business is hard, time-consuming and tiring. Also, the risk versus reward of chasing new business in hopes of something greater is slim.

If the win is there, take it. Do not overthink it. Double down until you have maximised every ounce of return from it. Only then look for the next version of this.

WHAT I WISH I HAD KNOWN

→ Start small and maximise every penny from every relationship!

→ Take time to identify and re-identify exactly who your target market is.

→ You are not trying to be the biggest. You just need to be the best for a select few that need you.

ARE YOU GOING TO SELL A PRODUCT OR DO YOU OFFER A SERVICE?

This sounds like a silly question.

It sounds like a basic, answerable question that will appear to serve no real purpose to you in setting up a business. You are probably asking, 'Why does this matter?' or thinking, 'Actually, I probably do a bit of both'. But it is of the utmost importance and can have a lasting impact on the success of your business.

Warren Buffett (probably the greatest living investor of our time) sums it up better than I ever could: 'Price is what you pay. Value is what you get.'

THE PRODUCT PITFALL

The reason it is crucially important is because if you sell a product, you are almost always dictated by price. This means your product, no matter how amazing, is restricted by the value people think it is worth or by other competitors' selling price. By definition a product serves a purpose. There is a value attached to this purpose and so a price people are willing to pay. This, in the long run, affects the level of profit you are ever able to make.

Yes, there are elements of supply and demand that can help manipulate price. For example, rare or limited-edition items such as trainers or old cars can increase in value, but again, that is because there is a limited amount of that particular product ever available. Do not even get me started on bitcoin.

In almost every case of the small business entrepreneur, this is not your remit. I believe this is one of the biggest reasons for small companies going out of business or failing after an amount of time.

'To found a startup means to risk a high failure rate. Twenty percent of businesses fail in their first year and around 60 percent will go bust within their first three years.'

—FUNDSQUIRE

In his book *The Everything Store*, Brad Stone discusses all things Amazon, the perfect example for this chapter. As almost everyone is aware, they are the mass shopping store and Prime membership offering that probably one in three people reading this book is subscribed to. (According to Jeff Bezos, Amazon Prime had 200 million subscribers as of April 2021!)

What do you think they do? If you think they sell products, you are so wrong. The product itself is the byproduct of their service.

You have this great product. Let us say it is something completely innocuous, like toilet paper. You then think, 'Okay, where do people go to buy this type of product?' Of course Amazon is a great place to get buyers. So you go online and list your products, offer Prime delivery and accept the fees they charge for hosting. Well, guess what? There are three thousand other people doing the same thing!

So what is your unique selling point? Softer, more individual sheets, aloe vera–infused? Do you think people on Amazon really care to find this? No, it is about price.

So then I ask you, do you think you have the best buying power on that site compared to other sellers? Not even close! So all that happens is your margins get squeezed trying to compete.

By the way, this is before Amazon analyses their data and sees there is a huge market for toilet rolls and launches their own brand (which they do *a lot*). And guess what...*they* do not have to pay those fees!

The point I am making is that in every single market that competes on price, it is a bloodbath, and only the biggest and a few select others survive long-term. Supermarkets actively compete to show their lowest prices for their own brands in comparison to a rival, and they are behemoths.

It is a race to the bottom when it comes to price.

How do you value a service?

Why do you buy an iPhone? Or want to own a Ferrari? If the

answer is because you need a phone to make calls, send texts or take pictures, you will never buy an iPhone. If the answer is because you need a car to take you from A to B as a form of transportation, you will never buy a Ferrari.

Yet the iPhone is the single highest-margin product in the history of mass electronics. Why?

It is because Apple is selling you more than just the use of the phone. The phone is actually a byproduct of what you are buying. Apple is selling you the service of being able to protect your privacy in a world where more and more data is sold. They are serving you in presenting you as a discerning luxury goods owner that cares about how you are perceived. They are giving you a single place from which to access everything: your phone, wallet, satellite navigation, music collection, TV and newspaper in an offer rolled up into four and a half inches and half a centimetre thick.

Now, can you honestly quantify a price for that? Because they are telling you that you are willing to pay over £1,100 every two years for that 'service'.

I know if I asked almost every person under the age of thirty-five to give up their iPhone for a month in exchange for a standard phone and a substantial amount of money, most would outright say no on the spot. It is an extension of who they are and their identity and is an absolute necessity.

So do you still think Apple is just selling phones?

Why do people buy a Ferrari?

I bet if you asked every person that bought a Ferrari if they bought it for practicality, reliability or the mileage per gallon, not one person would say these were the reasons. Yet it is the most prestigious car brand in the world. Now, tell me the last time you saw them traditionally advertise for business?

The answer is that you have not, as they do not! Yes, they advertise their brand through Formula 1, but that association with speed and sporting performance has always been their identity.

People buy a Ferrari because they know when they drive it, other people will look and, to an extent, judge. They know that they will, by association, be seen as discerning, of great taste, of significant wealth. Have you ever seen a Ferrari in the flesh? It is a work of art. It is a collector's item that increases in value the longer you have it, in many cases.

Yet you still think Ferrari sells cars?

There is a scene in *Gone in 60 Seconds* with Nicolas Cage that sums this up perfectly.

Nicolas Cage plays the character Memphis in this scene.

> **Memphis:** I've been in LA for three months now. I have money, I have taste. But I'm not on anybody's 'A' list, and Saturday night is the loneliest night of the week for me.
>
> **Roger the Car Salesman:** Well, a Ferrari would certainly change that.
>
> **Memphis:** Perhaps, mmm. But, you know, this is the one (points

at a Ferrari). Yes, yes yes...I saw three of these parked outside the local Starbucks this morning, which tells me only one thing. There's too many self-indulgent wieners in this city with too much bloody money! Now, if I was driving a 1967 275 GTB four-cam...

Roger the Car Salesman: You would not be a self-indulgent wiener, sir... You'd be a connoisseur.

Memphis: Precisely. Champagne would fall from the heavens. Doors would open. Velvet ropes would part.

At my previous company, they had a group of businesses. Some were dictated by price and others by service. And you know what?

The ones based on service were highly profitable, and the others eventually made a loss.

When it came to setting up my business, I made sure that everyone internally knew we were selling a service. Fundamentally, on paper, I was selling a collection of products to an end user. But what those products represented was convenience, return on investment, minimising risk, and affordable luxury. Once you can sell on service, you can control your pricing.

WHAT I WISH I HAD KNOWN

→ Long-term, a service offering is more profitable and less risky than selling on price.

→ Selling on price strips away all the added value a small business can offer.

→ You cannot quantify added value into a singular price, so you can charge whatever you want, as long as someone is willing to pay it.

DAVID VERSUS GOLIATH

YOUR STRENGTHS AS A SMALL BUSINESS

'The phrase "David and Goliath" has taken on a more popular meaning, denoting an underdog situation, a contest where a smaller, weaker opponent faces a much bigger, stronger adversary.'

—WIKIPEDIA

If that does not sum up what you are undertaking, I do not know what does. But you know what? Being a small company is fantastic. And do not let a competitor's size deter you.

David won, after all!

All the elements that drove me mad when I was part of something bigger were the opposite when setting up my own business. All you have to do now is maximise these traits to the fullest.

It is important before you start to have a sound knowledge

of the benefits of a small company. This is to give you a basic understanding of what to emphasise to make your business a success. You very rarely hear of the strengths of a small business; you just hear the negatives, normally as a bigger company steps into an area with more power and money.

STRENGTHS OF A SMALL BUSINESS

It is my job in this book to try and give you an edge with what you have available to you. Do not worry; for the underdog hoping to build something, being lean in size gives you some real strengths that benefit you.

BEING NICHE

The world, minus the few behemoths such as Amazon and Apple, is heading in a more specialised direction. The lockdown meant that more and more people tried to start up something unique to them. Everything from OnlyFans (it may not be to your taste, but they have maximised a niche) to Clubhouse to TikTok and Etsy has allowed people to show and offer themselves doing something unique and attract a wider audience than has ever been possible before without going through a 'gatekeeper'. Never before could you offer only red-coloured clothes or anime picture cushions, for example, and be able to target a big enough market to make it worthwhile. Now people are crafting huge followings and revenue doing this. There is no limit to the unique and wonderful individualised offering you can sell.

Did you know there are over a dozen companies selling edible shoes?

Bet your idea does not sound so mad now.

How about sending rotten flowers to an ex? There is a business that specialises in selling decaying flowers to people who broke up with you. I bet your confidence is growing now. If it is not, it should be, as I doubt your business is anywhere as niche as that.

For big companies, these niche, smaller groups of potential customers are just far too tiny a target market to spend their time and effort on when they have huge revenue numbers to hit. To think Amazon started by only selling books, and in a normal person's world, even that could be classed as a mass market for me or you.

It is estimated that there were 48.5 million books being sold on Amazon as of 2020.

One word—wow!

FLEXIBILITY

This applies across many facets of your business. Your decisions are not dictated by layers of hierarchy and procedures.

Need to source something for a particular client? Easy. Go and find it if it helps you win a deal. Need to spend that bit more time personalising an order? Easy. Take the time to package it up and write those extra emails specific to that customer. Need to deliver something the same day just because to you it is important? Go for it. It is your van and your time. Do with it what you want.

Big companies are dictated by the structure that has been implemented by their size and growth. Yes, it is perceived as efficient (although when you really look at it, it is not at all), but it is rigid. Use this to your advantage.

PERSONALISATION

You have the opportunity to know your client fundamentally better than any big company can. You have the ability to spend more time understanding their needs and concentrating on making sure they are wholly satisfied. No matter how hard a bigger company tries to ensure their customers feel special, there is a direct correlation between number of customers and levels of attention. You have the ability to make them feel so special that no one else can compete. Big companies would kill for this ability. Make it count.

'Eighty-four percent of consumers say being treated like a person, not a number, is very important to winning their business.'

—SALESFORCE

ADAPTABILITY

You have the ability to change direction or focus almost immediately.

In the tech world, this is famously called pivoting. You do not need approval or to analyse data before submitting a proposal on an idea. The companies that have stalled during the pandemic failed to act quickly enough to the change in business environment the world faced. You can change on the spot. (I am not saying this is recommended without some thought, but the ability is there.)[7]

A certain item or service is not working or well-received? Change it.

A certain line is selling well and leading you into a new area for the business? Test it on a small scale to see if it works.

The risk versus reward levels are much better weighted to smaller companies. Move fast to maximise the return, and move fast to minimise the loss.

There are so many great examples of successes and failures of this during the pandemic alone that I could write a book solely on this topic: Large companies that went bust by not adapting or by relying on old models that no longer work. Upstart companies that thrived with the sudden change.

A small company's success is filling the gaps that cannot and do not want to be filled by the big boys. Concentrating on these four points will give you direction and focus to maximise it.

But there is a catch.

STRENGTHS OF A BIG BUSINESS

There are also a number of strengths of big businesses (and correlating weaknesses associated with smaller businesses)

---

7   Ellen Huet, 'The Pandemic Pivot: How Three Startups Transformed during Covid', Bloomberg, August 4, 2021, https://www.bloomberg.com/news/articles/2021-08-04/ pandemic-pivot-how-table22-curative-welcome-transformed-during-covid.

that you need to be aware of and ensure you are prepared for. It would be naive to not highlight them (even if they are obvious) to ensure you do not play by the bigger companies' rules. If you do, they will metaphorically absorb all the oxygen in the room and leave you nowhere to go.

BUYING POWER

This is a recurring point throughout the book, as it is one of the largest factors affecting your continued success. Large companies have more cash than you, buy more stock than you and can set their prices lower than yours for longer than you can. Do not compete.

In a business based on price, it is like playing against the house in Vegas. Eventually you will always lose. You may win short-term, but I promise you will lose in the end. In order to negate the effects of price, you need to sell services that are not quantifiable. Added value, service, personalisation, individuality. These you can assign a price to that cannot be matched.

MARKETING POWER

The larger you are, the more people you need to target to grow. At some point, you cannot reach people organically (through word of mouth and recommendation) and have to pay to reach people. Make sure you maximise the free option first before trying to spread the word. As a small company, the best marketing is the people you already know and have sold to.

DIVERSIFICATION

Eventually, when you have maximised a product in a market-place, in order to grow, you need to offer a second product or an addition to the original to further expand. Apple went from the iMac to the iPod to the iPhone to the Apple store to the iMac and iPad to the iWatch and AirPods. (Let alone the Pro versions of many of these products and the purchase of Beats and introduction of Apple TV.)

You, as a small business owner, do not have the cash flow, the staff or the capacity to spread yourself thin. You need to concentrate on refining the one product or service you have and make it the best. You will make more money that way than ever trying to compete in multiple markets at once, chasing the money. As mentioned previously, I got greedy and tried it once. It was one of my biggest mistakes.

Again, the answer is do not compete. You will lose. Be yourself, concentrate and maximise the 100 percent effort in an area that bigger competitors are not as committed to as you. In the long run, you will either win or they will probably try and buy you.

WHAT I WISH I HAD KNOWN

→   Sell on service, not on price.

→   Your existing clients are your best marketing tool for growth.

→   Concentrate on one singular service and be the absolute best at it.

→   Find a specialist area and be the best at it.

→   Adapt to the marketplace as quickly as possible. First-person advantage has lots of short-term benefits.

→   Know your clients and make their experience better than anything else out there.

PART II
THE BEGINNING

So, you have gone through my mental, emotional and practical rollercoaster of what it takes to set up your own business.

Now you are set up and ready to go.

Full steam ahead.

Here we go...

YOUR FIRST DAY

ARE YOU READY?

The first day is both the most exciting and most anticlimactic day of the whole business life cycle. It is like your first day at school or your first kiss. The buildup is everything.

You have finalized your checklist (see previous lesson); you have your suit dry-cleaned and shirt pressed. Your shoes are polished, and in my case, it is the one and only time I am wearing matching socks. You have set numerous alarms to get up extra early (as early equals productive, supposedly), and you have even eaten a special breakfast.

You are 'the man' (or woman), and this is the first day of the rest of your life. Now what?

The buildup and prep to your first day is so different from the actual doing. It is like saying you are going to write a book (case in point: this book that took so damn long) or lose five kilos. You can do all the prep in the world and be as prepared as you can. You can have a double-sided piece of paper with chapter ideas or five different gym programs and two kilograms of protein powder ready to consume.

But if you do not actually start writing, or do not actually start training, it means nothing. Having a great company name, brand, and exciting website is all good and the foundation for something great, but if no one ever goes to your website or knows who you are, it is all a waste.

If on your first full day, you are not full of nerves and insecurities, then you do not want it enough. That sounds harsh, but it is true. It is a life-changing moment and an overall opportunity to make one of the biggest differences for yourself and for your family's future prosperity. You should be filled with excitement and self-doubt.

You should be second-guessing every new customer's reaction to what you are about to be offering, bracing yourself for the worst and hoping for the best.

But none of this means anything if you do not get out there. So many people get to the point of real-world application (doing it) and bail, even though they have done all the hardest parts.

Every single person is worried about how they will be judged. I was no different. You are no different. I look back on my initial brand and brochure, and it is diabolical. (No, honestly, it is an internal joke with my team.) I had no external business designing it, just myself, but I needed it, and I got it done in two weeks.

And you know what? Not a single customer stopped working with me because my brochure looked like some eighties school presentation or my business card font was twenty times too big, so you could see my name from across the room. It is all in your head. Concentrate on what you are actually offering. The rest is noise.

Now, a number of clients chose not to work with me on the first day due to the lack of trust in a new company or due to my pricing structure; they balked at my track record or my lead time. But these are addressable issues you would expect to come across if you stood in their shoes and looked at yourself.

The point is day one...it is time. It is time to get out there and do it. No excuses. It comes down to how much you want the business to be a success. To quote Dory from *Finding Nemo*, which is the strangest but most perfect example for a film geek like me, you have to 'just keep swimming', and this is the first day of forever doing this. If you do nothing else for the life cycle of your company, just do this and you will be fine.

WHAT I WISH I HAD KNOWN

→ There is no alternative to just doing. No amount of theory will give you practical results.

→ Make the most of your first day. It sets a precedent for you moving forward.

→ Image, in 99 percent of jobs, is nothing. Substance is everything.

WHAT DOES THE END OF YOUR FIRST WEEK LOOK LIKE?

It is the end of the first week. Thank fuck for that! If you are not dead on your feet and mentally a zombie, you did not leave it all on the field. If you are like me, I hope you hit the ground running.

You passed the fear of the first-day stage and targeted a list of people you had jotted down on your notepad or in your Excel spreadsheet. Now please tell me you are beyond excited at this point, and it has gone better than you had hoped.

If, like me, you targeted your list to death and hopefully a few people answered your call, returned your email, let you in their building and even found the time to meet you—that is a win.

The end of this week is one of the most important moments in the whole small business venture—a chance to assess real-world feedback.

No matter how well you know your product or service, your pitch is going to be rusty at best or like a toddler learning to take their first steps at worst. You will have rushed your phone calls, struggled for breath in the meeting rooms and probably muddled and clumsily reached your punchlines with almost every person.

You will have also gotten a real gauge, in the hullabaloo of mixed messages you were sending out, as to whether there is a real market for what you are offering. Or, more importantly, if your offering on paper is better or more unique than what they already have.

If a single customer comes back with friction, this is gold dust to your future success. Whether it is price, service, unique selling point, credibility or finances, every single meeting and feedback is king. There is no rejection that does not help you—as much as it will sting.

The best one that got me was on my second day; they said they wanted me to have a stronger track record (knowing I was a startup) before they could use us. My argument, amongst others, was that in order to have a track record, I needed customers like him to give us a go. The ultimate catch-22 scenario. Either way, he was not budging, so I knew when I pitched to other people to get ahead of this when streamlining my pitch.

WHAT I WISH I HAD KNOWN

→   Your pitch is average. Learn from the many attempts at doing it to fine-tune it and make it slicker.

→   Feedback is king. Not just now, but always. Never be too arrogant to listen to feedback.

→   Every rejection is better than an order at this stage. It tells you where to be. Make sure you listen.

WHAT DOES YOUR ROLE AS CEO REALLY ENTAIL?

In a small business of yourself and a few select people, the role of the CEO is pretty much everything. You step into every role that needs help, you drive sales forward, you deliver the product if needed and so on and so forth. This, for a lot of people, will be the whole brief of the CEO experience (depending on the evolution of the company)—and that is fine. To be as proactive as you can be, however, a large percentage of that time will be reactive to the immediate needs of the business.

However, at some point you need to reconsider your role if you are to have more employees and truly want to drive the business forward, even on a small scale.

So what is the next step?

In a nutshell, the role moves from 'thinking about what needs to be done by me' to 'hiring someone to do it'.

If you continue to think about the future success of the business and do not want to be in this position again, asking this exact question, you need to implement people in roles to solve the problems of the business.

Need to drive a business forward in sales?

Your whole focus is to find the best salesperson you can get for the money, train them and make sure they understand the business as well as you can possibly explain it. Mentor them when they need help, then let them get the hell on with it and move on to the next area that needs addressing.

Need to drive your website and marketing forward through social media?

Guess what? Find the best marketing person you can get for the money, train them and make sure they understand the business as well as you can possibly explain it. Mentor them when they need help, then let them get the hell on with it and move on to the next area that needs addressing.

You get the point.

So many small business owners (a) think that the way to get stuff done is to do it themselves to save money and (b) think that finding someone to do it is more hassle than undertaking it themselves. Both are huge falsehoods and can bring down a business.

Why? That lost time is priceless. To start, if you are constantly driving sales and meeting people, how can you possibly concentrate on improving the customer service experience? How can you deal with delivery issues? You cannot. You cannot be everything to everyone. Rather, you will end up being nothing of any use to anyone.

Second, if you want your business to be a market leader, even in a small market, why would you let an amateur (yourself) attempt to do things you have no idea how to do?

The number of small businesses you look at online and their website looks like a kid's school project is ridiculous. In a world based on international first impressions (the World Wide Web), how do people still allow this to be the standard they accept for themselves to save a few pounds?

Ask yourself how many websites you have clicked on and then clicked off when you saw how badly they were put together? Almost all independent food takeaway companies do exactly this.

Another great example of this is barbershops. It appears that the industry standard of barbershops in the twenty-first century is to have a collage of black-and-white photos of models with 'Fonzie-style haircuts' stuck to their windows. This is an old reference even for me!

Yet their target market is, I assume, any man eighteen years old and upwards. Even the people who remember those haircuts are now too old to want those cuts or, ironically, to have enough hair to request them. These shops eventually, like the dinosaur or the Sony Walkman, will become extinct.

It is your job as CEO to bring all the experts together to create something better than what they can do individually. To give them an environment that they will thrive in professionally and, if all goes well, financially. If you have recruited successfully, it is your job behind the scenes to create a company that maximises their strengths and minimises their weaknesses. If you have an expert on digital marketing who is skilled with computers, why get them involved in logistical procedures?

Do you have a person who thrives working from home on their own and who is far more productive at home than in an office? Stop dragging their arse ninety minutes each way to an office to get 60 percent of the output.

The whole point of a small business is having the flexibility to adapt. Flexibility also highlights another important lesson. COVID-19 has brought new issues to the forefront of businesses. One of these is the necessity of adapting.

Big world events have a knack for bringing future ideas forward or fast-tracking defunct or ancient procedures to the shelves of libraries. It is your job as a current CEO to try and navigate as quickly and efficiently as possible what is best for your company and where your industry is heading.

For example, when people could not go out, streaming companies saw a boom in viewership. Will it drop eventually? Possibly. But for a cinema chain, is the cinema experience good enough to bring people back to the same levels as they were before? I massively doubt it.

The cinema experience has not evolved anywhere near as much as the home cinema improvements to TVs, sound systems and quality. Yes, the chairs can recline, but what else has improved the experience? Not the £7 popcorn, that is for sure!

Add in the fact that COVID-19 has shoved convenience in the face of almost every customer to highlight this. Actually watching films in the comfort of my own home on a fifty-five-inch TV with my own bathroom and reasonably priced snacks, not being surrounded by strangers, is rather appealing.

Last, the four main players producing content now have a vested interest in circumnavigating the distribution stage of the cinema.

Will some chains survive? Of course. I personally love the cinema. But I am also happy to wait for certain films to hit Disney+, and I have Amazon Prime and Netflix as well.

So what is your business going to look like in the mid- to long term after this?

In both of my two areas of specialty services, we have designed them so they are as low admin-centric as possible. Although our software is basic (but cheap and suitable), we have designed our systems to allow my creatives to create. We have a specific detail-oriented person picking up the slack at the back end.

In my specialist sales team, we try to design it so that a deal can be closed and handed over in under thirty minutes and then taken off their hands all the way to delivery. This allows me to maximise the return from the skills they have without having to hire. It is not perfect, but the amount of admin (bullshit) I had to deal with just to close a deal at my previous company was just a huge waste of money and resources.

Finally, in your role, once you start recruiting, you have to start looking to the mid- and long term. If the short term is looking after itself, it is on you to direct and drive the future direction of the company. Reactive companies are normally already too late. You need to envision the future for the business so you can start taking steps now to get there.

WHAT I WISH I HAD KNOWN

→ The CEO's job is not to be the expert of everything. It is to be the expert in bringing specialists together for a greater sum of their parts.

→ Identify strengths and put in place the opportunity to maximise those. Do not waste the small amount of resources you have.

→ You cannot just be reactive. You need to reach a point where you are planning the future of the business, whether that is growth, diversification or even streamlining, should it be needed. These decisions should never be reactionary.

→ Change has happened quickly. Make sure you are assessing the impact on your industry.

→ Prepare to adapt.

→ Is there a new niche with which you can thrive?

THE IMPORTANCE OF CUSTOMERS LOVING (*NOT JUST LIKING*) YOUR COMPANY

If I asked you to list all the restaurants you 'like' going to, how many do you think you could write down? I could probably name thirty plus with a bit of time.

What if I asked you to write down who your favourite actor was or who your favourite sports star was? I bet you could do that in an instant.

Now imagine your customer is being asked by a friend about your company. Do you think they *loved* the service they received? Or did they just *like* it? Do you think they will remember you in six months if asked for a recommendation?

This is the biggest fundamental difference.

People *love* the iPhone, their Tesla and the series *Game of Thrones*. The experience those products give them is more than what an equivalent product does.

Have you ever asked one of these people who love these products about them? They *cannot* wait to tell you about them. The little nuggets of info you do not think you know but they do? The character development and how they could relate, the new app that allowed them to do something new? The technology of the dashboard and how it is just a matter of time before it will be self-driving? We have all been there.

Now ask a Ford driver about their car. Or an LG phone owner about their phone. I am certain you do not get the same response on such a regular basis.

You should be striving for the love response, craving it even.

You may not feel the ripple effect from the love of what you do or sell, but it is there and will pay off in the long run. If you can create that love, you will almost definitely be a success.

I have mentioned previously that it is hard to offer a truly amazing product or service, no matter how small. If you strive hard enough and get it right, the benefits become almost unquantifiable. Recommendations, word-of-mouth comments, talking amongst friends, written reviews. I have felt the benefits of all of these.

I have an 'introducer' to my business. (*An introducer is a person that does not actually order from us but puts customers in front of us through recommendations.*)

In the past five years, she has passed over two hundred clients to us who have ordered from us. (*She is technically one of our top five most important customers, and she is just one person.*)

That is not even the real win.

She has moved companies three times in that period. On every occasion, she was such an ambassador for us that when she left, all her colleagues continued to use us from then on, plus her new companies she went to work for also started to use us. That one person's network effects are hard to put an actual value on.

People who love you are priceless. Find as many as you can. I would trade fifty clients that like us for one person who loves us.

WHAT I WISH I HAD KNOWN

→ Strive to make customers fall in love with your offering.

→ Maximise the return from these people, as they do not come along very often.

→ Aim to convert the people who like you into people who love you. I promise it will be worth it.

WHAT IS YOUR WORK-LIFE BALANCE LIKE IN THE EARLY YEARS?

Let me clear this up nice and quick. There is not a work-life balance! This could be the end of the shortest lesson in history. This is the fundamental sacrifice you make when starting down this path.

You can pretend there is one, be upset at times when others do not work as hard as you, but the sooner you come to terms with the fact that you signed up for this, the better. It is an unwritten truth, and the quicker you accept it, the easier it will be for you to evolve 'how you work' to at least manage it.

In the first year, you are Mr Marketing and Mrs Delivery and even King Product.

Nothing should leave your business without it being to a standard you expect. Your attention to detail is everything and sets the benchmark. However, I am not going to lie; this approach is great for growing your business but not so great for your home life, family life, friendships, intimacy and everything in between.

The more open you are with your partner about this, the better chance you have for coming up with a system that is bearable for both of you. I want to say 'one that works for both of you', but that would just be a lie. Fundamentally, what you are doing is selfish. It is prioritising your career above everything else, within reason—at least in the short term.

It is no different from a superstar athlete sacrificing dinners out and nights out for a good night's sleep, warm-weather training and boring, nutritionally packed meals day in and day out.

Finding that system is trial and error for every person.

For me, once a year for a week, my wife and I have an agreement to go away somewhere hot, just the two of us, all-inclusive, and recharge our batteries, both mentally and physically. The location is irrelevant, really, as long as it is hot and serves cocktails and beer throughout the day. The kids stay with grandparents or friends for the week (which they love, as they get spoiled rotten), and we have a friend house-sit for our dogs and cats. As tough as it is, we have learnt to accept this as guilt-free as possible for the good of our relationship, and, in turn, it filters down into the good of our overall home and work life for the rest of the year.

However, it was not always like this, and I learnt the hard way. Years previously, I was travelling to Southeast Asia from the months of January to March and then September to November, as this was where the business was (in a nutshell). As I hated being away from the family too long, I flew out on Virgin Atlantic every Wednesday night on the night flight to Hong Kong. As soon as I landed, I went out with clients that evening for 'entertaining'.

For the next three days, I worked from 10:30 a.m. to 7:00 p.m. in exhibitions and product launches, came back to my room for no more than ninety minutes, tried (and failed) to go to the gym, showered, changed and went out for the night, resulting in most evenings finishing after 2:00 a.m.

At the end of the Sunday exhibition at 7:00 p.m., I got changed in the exhibition room (as I had checked out that morning), went straight to the airport and boarded an 11:30 p.m. flight back home that landed at London Heathrow between 5:00 and 6:00 a.m. I was home by 8:00 a.m., ready to take my boy to school that morning.

In hindsight, this was in no way healthy. My wife and I missed each other. I missed my birthday in November three years in a row (which bothered her). I missed so many social events I cannot even count. My skin was literally grey through lack of sunlight, being in hotel lobbies and convention halls with no natural light. I was sleep-deprived due to the long nights, time differences and alcohol, and my body was crying out for vegetables.

This went on solidly for four years. At the end of the 'season' in year three, I had done ten weekends on the spin. This was ridiculous, even for me (did I mention it was economy class?).

I had it down to a well-oiled machine. For every facet of the trip I had my routine, but even I was absolutely broken. See the film *Up in the Air* for the perfect example of the routine.

Even by my standards and the 'it is for the good of our long-term future' and 'it will really benefit us in a few years' time', this really took the piss. I was so hungry to be a success that my wife's concerns for me were annoyances; rather than understanding (the impact of my work success was paramount), I dismissed her worries without concern. Deep down I knew I was broken, but it was an agreed sacrifice in my mind.

However, to try and make amends (wow, it sounds laughable now), we agreed to a trip to the Maldives on the day I landed back from Asia. I came home and showered; my wife had pre-packed me a case with educated clothing suggestions. I landed at 5:30 a.m. at Heathrow Terminal 3 and was back at Heathrow Terminal 2 by midday—just nuts, is it not?! In my mind this was different, though, as it was a personal holiday and a way to repair the sacrifices we had both made the past three months, every Wednesday to Sunday night.

But of course, because I had no boundaries or limits, nothing really changed.

Imagine paradise. By day two on the beach, not a person either side of us to be seen, on this picturesque island with drinks in our hands, I was meant to be soaking up some rays and unwinding. But of course I was on my iPad answering emails instantaneously as they came in. The first day, my wife was understanding and *let it slide*, as she knew there would be fallout and follow-up from the weekend(s) just gone and loose ends that would need tying up. (Honestly I cannot stress enough how much I took advantage back then.)

But at that point, she reached her limit...and it was the best thing that happened to us.

Her argument revolved around how much is enough.

And what was the point of working so hard for the last ten weeks / three years if this did not earn me the opportunity to take a week off? Was it that I was a control freak, so had to be involved in everything? That the world would stop functioning if I did? And last, what is the worst that could happen if I did not look at my phone? All of these were completely valid questions and annoyingly made complete sense. I hated it when she was right.

My first reaction was to be defensive, with counter-arguments that had pseudo-logic to justify my claims. But deep down I knew the grey area of balance had been completely eroded. More importantly, I knew that, for all the reasons listed above, it could not be kept up. So I had to find a solution that made it more manageable.

I am not going to sugarcoat it. It has been trial and error, but with mobile phone technology and a well-run business it is a lot easier, as a lot less goes wrong. But for the sake of all things holy, at that point I had to change.

Now we have an understanding that works for both of us.

I wake up and check my emails. Due to the time difference in the Caribbean (where we try to go for all-inclusive holidays), the UK workday is almost done. I sort through the important ones and forward the others. But above all, I make sure I have read all of them so I can keep my anxiety in check.

We go to breakfast and head to the pool and do not return until lunch. After lunch, I return to my room and spend five minutes again scanning my phone. Normally there is no more than a handful of emails and spam.

Around 5:00 p.m., we normally call it a day and head back to the room. My wife chills out / naps / starts getting ready for dinner at 7:00-ish.

At that point, I get an hour. That hour is mine to do as I wish in regards to work. It gives me the opportunity to reply to the more complex emails that need my response. It allows me to give direction for the next day to team members and gives me the opportunity to do any free writing that I wish to do. By the time the weekend comes, this hour is not needed, as few work emails or WhatsApps are coming in, so it becomes purely enjoyable work that I am choosing to do.

Ironically, I have found out that when I am relaxed, I do all my forward thinking for the future of the business—who knew relaxing could help this?

Now, I know this is not perfect. I am not pretending it is completely healthy. But it works for me. It works for my wife, and it is the balance and agreement we have in place. This has now worked across different holidays and different time zones in the world.

The point of the story is find the balance that works for you.

WHAT I WISH I HAD KNOWN

→ The business is all-consuming. Embrace it, but communicate.

→ Take time to assess when it is getting out of hand. It may benefit you in the short-term, but long-term it could affect both your home life and your work life.

→ Find a system that works, whether at home or away. Once you do, it becomes routine and helps you manage yourself better. The business will continue to consume you until you stop it.

IS DOING THE EASY THINGS ACTUALLY EASY?

Do not believe the old adage that doing anything easy is *actually* easy. It is deceptively hard.

People always worry when setting up a business that what they want to do or the idea they have is so simple that people must be doing it and doing it well. This could not be further from the truth.

In most industries, there are a few people (at most) that are doing it really well, a few more that do a satisfactory job and then a whole heap of rubbish businesses that have lived off past successes or old ways. All of the varying levels of successful businesses mentioned above can still be improved on—and they should be trying to every day. You need to remember (if you have listened to my earlier advice on why to set up your business) that you must, deep down, believe you can do it better than what has gone before or what is currently out there.

There are of course exceptions to this rule, such as industries that require huge financial backing to break into, even if the premise is easy. I would not recommend trying to take on Amazon, Netflix and Apple in the streaming wars, for instance. But then again, if you are reading this book, it is not because your aim is to be a multinational media conglomerate.

In my industry, the business I run, on paper, is easy. But the amount of competitors I assessed and studied before taking the leap that could not do the basics right was astounding.

My first real-world example:

> My aim is to deliver a collection of products in one day, all at the same time. Sounds easy. Then add in that these items are all coordinated at the same time to complete an overall offering from different suppliers. Still sounds easy.
>
> The items individually are just that: items. But when brought together on one day at one time, they create something more—they create a unique offering.
>
> Can it be done by an individual? For sure. Would it involve a lot of time sourcing and being there for multiple deliveries? Definitely. What happens if it goes wrong? More time and more money.
>
> Then add in that we build the items and finish off the dressing to complete an overall look.
>
> Again, could they do it cheaper if they really searched? Yes. After all, as mentioned earlier, there is always a company that will sell a product cheaper if you search hard enough.
>
> Does a person really want to do it? For their own home, where they are willing to wait for the 'right' item and it is a 'work in process' (two terms my wife has used when designing our home)? I know I would and have.

What if they were then on a deadline linked to a financial return based on a property they have bought? What price is their time worth? What price could you attach to solving a unique problem that can be solved in thirty minutes using a specialist company that could reduce your wait time by 50 percent if you did not do it yourself?

Suddenly, I am solving a real-world problem with financial consequences. I am saving the customer time and money in the short term, as I can deliver it more quickly and more conveniently.

How many people can go to the supermarket and buy dog food? Almost everyone. Then why do I buy it from Amazon? Saving of time, probably money and, above all, convenience.

People will pay huge sums of money to save time and for convenience. They will pay for the most basic of services and products for this exact reason. If they did not, then paying gardeners to cut your lawn or people to wash your car would not exist. Both tasks are relatively easy to work out with minimum financial outlay. Yet there are thousands upon thousands of these services nationally.

WHAT I WISH I HAD KNOWN

→ Do not be deceived; most companies are average at best at what they do. Analyse where they are weak and be better.

→ Even the simplest of tasks can be a worthwhile market.

→ The ability to save someone time or money or give them convenience is massively underrated.

WHAT ABOUT THE BIG WIN?

'What about the big win? You mean the one where we all sail off into the distance with yachts and boob jobs?'

The title of this chapter and the quote above are from Will Smith's character, Nicky Spurgeon, in *Focus*. (It is a great film; you should see it.) Every time I watch it, I cannot help but laugh in hindsight. Every single person dreams that this will happen to them. I assume it is the same feeling felt by the people who play the lottery, who think this weekend could be theirs, retirement is about to hit, or a Ferrari is going to be on their driveway. Deep, *deep* down, we all hope.

Everyone is looking for the once-in-a-lifetime deal. The big unicorn of a project or opportunity where you can sail off into the sunset. The one where you go out and buy an expensive car or pay off your mortgage, the one where all your hard work has paid off and you can take your foot off the pedal or the one that will define you as the success you see yourself as...

Yeah, that does not exist! And do not say cryptocurrency…

It is a myth. A fabrication of the movie industry and unscrupulous people to make money. The get-rich-quick scheme for the entrepreneur. Trust me, we have all been there, and we have all thought about what we would do in the situation.

I know for a fact I have had a deal so big and so close to closing that I could almost taste it, and I promise, in my head I had already spent the profits.

Very early into our company, a project presented itself, and I really thought it was ours to win. Of course, in the end we did not, and I was demoralised for a good week. I saw it as a game changer for me and my company (but mostly for me, if I am being brutally honest). It became almost a badge of honour that this company was going to give us the business even when we definitely were not the right company for it.

I foolishly believed that my sales pitch was so good that I had convinced a customer that we were part of the big time and worthy of their business.

Deep down I knew this was a borderline form of deception, but for a short while, it did feel good. Reputable people and companies want to work with other proper people and companies. Like me, I can see through someone trying to take the shortcut or not being committed to something (we all have that friend that has tried several businesses for a short time for the quick fix). They carry a stench of falseness and short-termism. It is almost a nervous energy that they are going to be found out. An energy you have never seen in a confident person with proper credentials.

Trust me, you do not want this deal. I promise. This deal makes you think you are further along than you are. That you deserve it. That you are better than you are. Your whole mindset changes for the worse. You lose your hunger, like when a boxer gets comfortable as a champ, losing the desire that he had when he was the challenger.

'The worst thing that happened to you, that can happen to any fighter: you got civilized.'

—MICKEY GOLDMILL, *ROCKY III*

Guess what? Sooner or later, he gets knocked out by the younger, hungrier challenger. In this case, you lose to your former self.

The best thing in the long run is to not believe these deals are yours to win early on or try and win them at all. (Wait for my rationale.) It is much better to graft every deal and every customer as if it is your last. To iterate and iterate and change and edit to perfect your craft or offering. This will serve you so much better in the long run.

But the truth is, those deals do not happen for people like us who are not ready. (I know, there is always the exception to the rule.) Those deals do not come off if you do not deserve them. I did not deserve it. I knew this. I had not earned it. We are sold this story that people have these career-changing deals or sales early on, but when you look deeper, you realise years and years of graft and networking go into putting yourself into a position to win it.

It is not just the product or the service. It is the psychology behind it. I knew deep down I did not fully deserve that deal (even if I tried to convince myself I was worthy). It is no different than when you first pitch your product to a normal customer or a comedian does their routine the first time, compared to when they are on stage at Madison Square Garden. By then, you are just psychologically better, more impressive, demanding of that success (even if you cannot quantify it) and ready for it.

When you are ready for those deals, they start to come to you.

WHAT I WISH I HAD KNOWN

→ Concentrate on the small deals. These pay the bills.

→ Do not go chasing the big life-changing deals. When you are ready, they will be presented to you.

→ Distraction into believing you are better than you are is a business destroyer.

PART III
CULTURE

Culture, to me, is the most important factor of the business I set up.

It underpinned everything I, and we as a company, stood for.

It underpinned every decision, every hire and every conversation.

Having been at a company and watching its culture disintegrate, I promised that it was one area that I would strive to be unwavering on.

If I were to sell today and someone asked me what I was most proud of, the company culture would be it. If you can craft a culture unique to your business and staff, you are almost invincible.

Culture is hard to describe and almost impossible to quantify. But the lessons shown in the coming pages will tell you more about me than any other area of the business.

I HATE LOSING...AND THAT IS OKAY

'I hate losing. I hate losing twice as much as I like winning!'

—BILLY BEANE, *MONEYBALL*

Anyone that is successful that says they do not mind losing a deal, or a hire, or seeing a rival company succeed is lying! And it is okay to feel like that.

I personally do not dwell on others' successes and genuinely wish them luck. I believe if they have won a deal, they did something better than I did. Whether that is the pitch, the networking or the product, somewhere down the line, they made the difference.

It does not mean you have to be happy about it.

The thing is, I know my team is great, I am half-decent at what I do and I am proud of what I have built, so a certain expectation of success comes with that. Very few times do I go into a business deal or transaction and say to myself, 'This is not ours to win' or 'You know what? We have not done enough preparation or work to deserve this'. So when we do win, I am obviously very happy—extremely happy in some cases, and grateful to everyone involved, as I could not have done it without them.

Deep down, if we have put the work in, I feel we deserved it. But because of the high standards I hold myself, my team, and my company to, the expectation that we will win comes with the territory. I set up the company to be the best, so when we win a deal a little bit of me is proven right.

Due to this expectation, the opposite applies when losing. I am not going to lie; it fucking stings, and it can ruin the next few hours of my day. Do not get me wrong; it is the best learning curve in the world (as mentioned before), it kicks you in the arse and it makes you reevaluate and reiterate what you have done to improve again...but this does not mean I have to like it!

No person or company wins every time. Just Google Usain Bolt at his first or last Olympics. Even Muhammad Ali's record is spattered with losses. But if you learn from them enough and the wins outweigh the losses, you will be fine.

Any self-respecting business owner works harder to improve their business straight after an important loss. It is your duty to over-analyse and overcompensate.

If you do not do it, who will? Brushing it off as just one of those things is a recipe for the fast track to bankruptcy.

WHAT I WISH I HAD KNOWN

→ Losing is the perfect time to evaluate and improve. Do not waste this opportunity.

→ Mourn it, be pissed off, but do not dwell on it. It is done. On to the next.

→ If you do not mind that you lost, ask yourself why.

IS THE DEAL EVER REALLY DEAD?

The answer is no. The deal is never dead.

This is both literal and a mindset. But for you, as a small business owner, it is an integral one to carry with you for as long as you run your business.

Can you actually lose a deal? Of course. But so much can be made or found from this loss. One of the mindsets I brought to the company is exactly this. We live and die by it.

LITERALLY—THE DEAL IS NEVER DEAD

Whenever we are told we have lost business, we go immediately on the offensive. Our approach is that until the money has been physically paid, the deal is still very much alive. In fact, in a couple of instances, even after it had been paid, we managed to salvage the deal.

A client telling us we have lost actually tells us nothing other than we have not done a good enough job in convincing them to this point that we are the right company.

Stage one is obviously to make contact with them and ask them why. If they come back to us, we know they are still on the hook and warm. We know we have an answer for any reason they might give, as we have been here before. Was it price? Easy. We can adjust or change products. Delivery time? I will find a slot sooner. We have not been around long enough, and you are worried about reputability? Please find a link to our Trustpilot and have two emails and a phone call from people linked to that deal telling you how amazing we are.

If we are going to lose it, we are going to make it as emotionally tiring as possible to find fault as a reason not to use us.

We have twice convinced buyers to get a refund from another company and helped them make the process of getting the money back as emotionally painless as possible, including giving them the email to send (the irony), so we could deal with them. These people were in time zones eight hours away, which made it a real pain in the arse, but we would not let it go.

Stage two (if they do not respond to us) is to work with the person who introduced them.

In our industry, a lot of the introducers are like gatekeepers and carry sway. What better way to lean on a client than through a trusted colleague? The colleague may be incentivised to do it, but who cares? I still believe we are the right people for the job; we just need them to know it.

FIGURATIVELY—THE DEAL IS NEVER DEAD

This is far more powerful than physically going after the lost business. That has a definitive period of strength until you can do no more. However, building a mindset in your team that you fight for everything and it is about wanting it more than others will run forever.

If everyone believes that we will not be beaten, it creates a drive and focus that competitors just cannot compete with. Willingness to go that extra mile and do those little things can change a business exponentially. Everyone bounces off of each other. Every meeting has an atmosphere of winners, of drive and clarity that you keep persevering.

I would say it is one of the most powerful drivers in my business and has crafted us into who we are today. No one sees it as a big deal. Losing anything is a waste of your time and effort, so going that extra little bit to give yourself a chance of success is priceless. No one can compete with it. If it is forced, you do not believe it deep down. Anyone that does not have it ingrained will be overwhelmed by trying to compete with this culture.

WHAT I WISH I HAD KNOWN

→ Do not take lost deals at face value. Kick the tyres to see if you still have time.

→ Losing a deal is a waste of everyone's time and effort. Putting in a few phone calls to try and salvage it is a small amount of time in comparison to what you put in.

→ Culturally believing you deserve to win and you will not accept it when you do not gives you unbelievable drive as a company.

ARE YOU A MERCENARY OR A MISSIONARY?

Before you even take your first steps into the business world, ask yourself a question: Why do you want to do this?

I could have listed this in the earlier part of the book addressing what to do before you get started, but it is so culturally important to who I was that I put it here.

This is one of the fundamental questions Jeff Bezos asks when looking into whether to purchase a company. For him, it is to delve into the motivations and main reasons for the person setting up and running the business in the first place. He argues there are two types of people.

The Missionary—'a member of a...group sent into an area to promote their faith or provide services, such as education, literacy, social justice, health care, and economic development'.

—WIKIPEDIA

By association, a person who is there to make a difference, to create change and in it for fundamentally the right reasons. They do not seek the rewards that come from their effort. There is a bigger picture than that. Personal gain is second to creating or doing something worthwhile.

The Mercenary—'primarily concerned with making money at the expense of ethics. A professional soldier hired to serve in a foreign army'.

—WIKIPEDIA

The reason I address this at the beginning is that there is an irony: in business, missionaries go on to be more successful than mercenaries. This is because it is the immeasurable factors that drive you to be successful.

If you do not love what you do, what is the motivation for your business to be better? When you have one of those really bad days (and trust me, there are loads), what is the fire that keeps you on the path to success? The drive to create something that you are proud of or that can make a difference digs you out of that hole. It tells you to go on just one more day or make one more call. It tells you that you can do better.

I am not saying being driven by money or fame does not work. For some people, that is the motivation, more than anything, that drives them. The issue is when the money or the fame does not come straight away; it is hard to be patient and wait for it. Success can take years. Are you willing to wait for that? There is a feeling of short-termism with mercenaries.

I was fortunate to know, after reading many famous stories, that success does not come overnight. I also had zero interest in fame or ego to show off my accomplishments. I still do not. There is nothing special about me; I just work hard and love what I do.

I can look back on some of the bad days where we had no money coming in or had lost a big deal and I really thought *fuck this—it is just not worth it*, but I knew this was superficial, as deep down, my reaction was because I really did care, and it stung me that I was in this position. The amount of people that start a business to make a quick buck and then, when it gets tough, move on to another idea because it is too difficult is very high. Everyone knows someone like this.

It is personal when you want to make a difference. It does sting when you lose a deal if you think you are the best because, fundamentally, they do not believe in you.

If you are in it for the money or the fame, my best bit of advice is stay where you are. Collect a salary without all the hassle that comes with being a business owner, and do it on the side. The amount of crap you have to deal with far outweighs the wins early on if you are in it for the money.

WHAT I WISH I HAD KNOWN

→ Statistically, you are more likely to be a success if you are in your business for the love rather than the money.

→ Wanting to make a difference is better motivation than any amount of money in the long run.

→ Be wary of the desire for instant gratification if you are looking to set up a new business—it does not exist.

SHOULD YOU CHOOSE PRINCIPLES OVER THE MONEY?

At a few key occasions throughout your tenure as a business owner, you are going to come across an internal dilemma: whether to choose money over morals. This decision is tougher than it seems (especially when times are tough), and how you deal with it can define you and the direction and culture of the business.

It might be working with someone with suspect practices, or a company who treats staff in the wrong way or is screwing someone in the deal you are part of. As a new business, this is a really tough spot to be in to take the right path.

When you are more established and have a steady cash flow and a recognisable brand, it is a lot easier to take the high ground and walk away. When you have bills to pay and it is the difference between broke and bonus, you really start to question yourself.

In my previous employment, being the largest in our selected industry meant we dealt with anyone. We were indiscriminate to background, principles and morals. It did not extend to Third World dictators, but it was not far off. The only discerning filter we cared about was the colour of money and how much they had. Now, I am not a moral-high-ground angel myself, and working in such a toxic environment when I was younger, I definitely took the easy deal and dealt with the dickheads more than I should have. My moral compass said that as long as the amount of shady individuals I dealt with was small, I could just about handle it.

That, and the money was good enough. This was considering the industry I worked in, where being a high-level arsehole seems a prerequisite to participate.

So when I set up the new company and was deciding on my culture and target customer list, obviously a lot of these came up in the quest for a viable business. I made it a point right at the start to blacklist nine or ten of these existing people and to never deal with them directly. To this day, I have not dealt with eight of them!

The two exceptions to this were that one of them left the industry (a win) and one of my team deals with another through a third party (less of a win). However, before this happened, I explained my stance on the individual in question to my team member and gave them my opinion but at the same time explained that they needed to come to their own conclusions. He is still a dick but only in the smallest doses, indirectly, and not affecting us.

However, about four months later, an opportunity arose

that involved a person on the blacklist. The deal was not a blockbuster, but it *was* a long-term opportunity for consistent business. For anyone at this early stage of their business, words such as *consistent* or *repeat business* are like the equivalent of hearing 'abracadabra' around a magician—you know something good is coming. It is what any business strives for, as it under-pins against your costs, and if you get enough, you know your month or year is going to be great before getting out of bed, as sales income is higher than total expenses (the dream for any company).

It was actually too big a decision for me to make myself. It sounds silly, does it not? But it was.

It had consequences either way—financial versus moral (and future decision impact). They always say after you break the rules once or cheat on a test, it is a bit easier to do it again, as you become desensitised to it. This is no different.

As it had a direct impact on our weekly, monthly and yearly business and projections, I put it internally to my business part-ner and externally to my wife for feedback. The ramifications on the next two or three years of the business, and in turn my home life, could be built on this, so I thought I owed it to them to hear their opinions on the matter.

To give context, at this stage we had fast-tracked our hiring process with outside funding, and we were growing our number of orders each month, but we were not making any real money, as our margin, buying power and history were low, so we were paying a premium. Deals were not consistent (to say the least), and like any new business, it was a slog! This deal would have underwritten the business at that point. However, I really, *really* disliked this person. He was top tier, king of arseholes and was manipulating the situation, knowing that we needed the business, and treating us accordingly—he knew he had the power. I played the game as much as I needed to but still was sticking to my principles to avoid dealing with him.

I was shocked at my business partner's response. He explained that money was really tight, but he was just one person, and he believed in us as a business and in what we were doing. We needed to have faith in our offering, and we had made a decision at the start of the business not to deal with people like this. To break one of our rules for the sake of short-term money woes was a bad-principle decision, and we would live to regret it.

My actual partner explained how the impact of these people at my previous company had worn away at me. We did not need them and should just believe for a bit longer and wait.

True to form, once we declined the opportunity to work with this person, he bombarded me with email abuse and phone calls telling me that I was an idiot, that I was naive and that the business would fail. And how he would tell everyone he knew not to work with us and we would come crawling back for his business.

With a really new business and living hand to mouth per month based on deals, obviously my stress levels did elevate. But deep down I knew this would be the right decision.

As it happens, the following month, we closed a really big deal that paid all our bills for three months. It is funny how things turn out. I have seen the person in question three times since then. He is on his third company, and I make a point of highlighting how well our company is doing each time. Childish, I know.

The point I want to communicate is that you are going to be put in a really tough position where you need to weigh up the right decision to make. I am not pretending that I made the right decision. Everyone's circumstances are different. I made the right call for the business and for myself at that particular crossroads.

WHAT I WISH I HAD KNOWN

→ When decisions have to be made between money and morals, money wins short-term and morals win long-term.

→ If in doubt, ask someone you trust or who understands your situation for their opinion. You may not agree, but it will give you a new perspective.

→ The harder the decision, the longer you should take to make it. There is no rush. Never regret your choices because you made them too quickly.

TAKING ACCOUNTABILITY FOR EVERYTHING

I have talked about it before, but at times in your tenure as an entrepreneur, it can be the most insular, mentally challenging, lonely place. It can make you question all your intuitions and decisions you have made, not just at work, but in every facet of your life.

Now, it is extremely hard for some people more than others to shake this vicious circle of self-deprecation and lack of motivation as it keeps coming, wave after wave.

What people never told me, though, was that no matter how much your partner, lover, mother or others tell you how well you are doing or how proud of you they are, it counts for nothing. You can appreciate their words and the good-luck card they sent you, but deep down you know their thoughts only scratch the surface.

What no one ever told me, and what I took a long time to learn being a business owner, is that it comes down to you and you only. It is daunting to hear, but it is harrowingly true.

The first step you have to take is to accept that as CEO, you take accountability for everything...and I mean everything. Gary Vaynerchuk talks about how you can be liberated by accepting this, that this mindset allows for no letdowns. It allows for no disappointment in anyone. It completely liberates you.

This appears hard to accept on the surface, as there are so many moving parts that you cannot control. You cannot possibly listen to every sales call from every team member and ensure they are saying what they should say. You cannot have possibly accounted for a supplier delivering goods late, ruining a relationship with a client. You could not have known your best client was going to leave the industry, leaving a hole in the business for sales.

Or could you?

If you reverse engineer it and lean into acceptance that you, solely, are responsible, your whole mindset shifts.

Was that salesperson the best person I could have hired? Had they had enough training so that the conversations were as effective as possible at doing their job?

I know from firsthand experience that members of my team promised things to people they should not have. Was I pissed off? Did I have to divert my time to step in and deal with it? Yes. But the real question is did I communicate the parameters of their role well enough to stop this from happening? The answer is obviously no. You could argue that some people are just stupid—which I strongly believe is true. But then it comes back to the 'who hired them?' question again.

Any company that has inventory has been let down and delayed by a supplier at some point. Post-COVID-19 and shipping container calamity, I would imagine 99 percent of people are in that boat (no pun intended).

Is that the supplier's fault? Yes, for not delivering when they said they would. But is it not my fault for rationing inventory so thin that I had no buffer and things had to go completely perfectly for the job just to be delivered? Did I not have a backup plan? Had I pre-warned the customer this might happen to manage expectations? Or, even better, did I allow a grace period between delivery and shipping to the customer just in case it was delayed? If the answer is no, it is on me.

Last, I share this example that happened to me personally. A fantastic customer left a job where we were their sole supplier. They gave us all their business, and their departure wiped the revenue off my future predictions almost overnight. A nightmare for any small business! The question I should have asked myself is 'Why did I leave the business in such a precarious position that one person's or company's business could almost fold my business?'

Where was the contingency plan? Where was the diverse selection of customers who all chip in to craft a consistent and well-rounded business model protected by variations?

Once you can truthfully accept this, all you need is belief

in yourself. Trust me, it soars inside you. It burns like a fire because you are not trapped, dictated or resentful of anyone. If you fail, it is completely on you. This mindset makes you look at every situation in a different light and reassess decisions. Sometimes these things happen at bad times, but if you truly accept them, you just brush them off and move forward to ensure they do not happen again, concentrating on the future and not dwelling on the past.

WHAT I WISH I HAD KNOWN

→ Accountability is liberating.

→ This mindset will take your business to the next level.

→ It takes some time to understand that it is not about punishing yourself but about giving yourself room for growth and development.

WHY YOU SHOULD NEVER MAKE THE SAME MISTAKE TWICE

From start to finish when setting up and running your own business, your execution from day to day will be littered with mistakes. You would not be human if this did not happen.

These mistakes will be a mix of disappointment, frustration, financial and emotional consequences (hopefully not long-lasting) and some of the biggest learning curves of your career. These are all, in the long term, super important and rewarding in making future you and your business a success—trust me!

However, making the same mistakes over and over again is a death sentence. What I have learnt from my firsthand experience along with senior people I have worked with at other companies is the ability to learn from my errors. This is extremely difficult for a lot of people for many reasons.

So why should people learn from their mistakes?

1. IT MEANS ACCEPTING THAT SOMETHING ACTUALLY WENT WRONG.

A *lot* of people love to pass blame (it is such a big thing it has its own name: blame culture). It means not taking personal accountability. If you do this long-term as a CEO of a business, it is a disaster. You never fully address the problem, so do not understand where the error occurred. This can affect culture, process and more. You are there to nip it in the bud and be a problem-solver.

Whether it is how a deal is lost, why a staff member left or, even more consequential, why you lost money, it needs to be addressed somewhere. Something went wrong and was done by somebody. Possibly you.

2. BY ACCEPTING BLAME, YOU ARE NOT A FAILURE.

You are going to fail hundreds of times. Failure is going to feel like part and parcel of life. Failure is not an issue and should be embraced, as mentioned before, not hidden behind. Confronting why you failed and how to learn from it is actually a weird win. The small business mentality is designed to be adaptable so you can quickly turn the negative event into a positive.

3. MAKING MISTAKES CAN COST YOU SO, SO MUCH MONEY.

Making any financial mistake, whether it is stock-related, staff-related or something else, has its consequences. You can recover in the short or mid-term from any situation once. If it happens again, this can result in all your working capital or profit for the year disappearing if the error is large enough.

Money will forever be a concern as a small business. Do not waste it unnecessarily.

WHAT I WISH I HAD KNOWN

→ Accept when you are wrong. Learn and move on.

→ Turn the negative into a positive.

→ Ensure financial mistakes are kept to a minimum. A couple of financial mistakes can break even the best small businesses.

PART IV

KEEPING COSTS DOWN

Costs can force the closure of even the most successful businesses.

Cost is a silent assassin that creeps up on you and takes you out without you seeing it coming.

Cost comes in many forms and is hard to judge before it is too late.

Costs are always higher than you think.

Costs, at different times, have almost cost me my business.

When sales are strong and business is successful, your cost base gets put on the back burner. In theory, if your sales keep on the current trajectory, you can afford better salaries, premises, expenses, fixed assets and so on. It is almost a natural evolution into 'needing' to spend more. Until sales slow down or you get a tax bill.

It is only then that you appreciate the small expenses. It is only then that you have to really examine what you are spending your money on.

Keeping your costs low is second only to keeping your profits high. The closer those numbers come together, the harder it gets.

OVERHEADS

YOUR PROFIT KILLER

Please repeat this or save this wisdom before you make any big decision, as it will save you a fortune: do not make the mistake of renting expensive premises! Overheads are a profit killer. Overheads are always more than you think or budget for.

One of the biggest overheads of any business other than salaries is office and warehouse space. The amount of people and industries I know that take luxurious showrooms and high-value premises to appear like they belong is beyond crazy. This is doubly stupid now, post-COVID-19 lockdowns, where the norm of coming to the office will never be the same again. I have two close friends who have lost everything due to long, expensive leases.

Do you need some form of office and warehouse space if you are going to run a business properly? Absolutely.

Do you need to take a long, hard look at where and how much you need? You are damn right.

This is, at a minimum, a five-year decision (based on lease length), so make sure you are certain!

My previous company had a showroom-office hybrid location off of Oxford Street in London. For anyone that does not know this place, it is the world-famous shopping street in London. It is prime space for selling to retail buyers, with luxury office space in its periphery. It is also a hub of the cool and wealthy.

It costs circa £400,000 a year, £30,000 on bills (estimated) and a full showroom refresh kit out at approximately £80,000 every eighteen months by the company.

So what did you get for that?

A floor of a lovely building in prime central London that all clients 'could get to'. Staff travelled in from all across London and the local counties to work from there either full-time or part-time depending on the role. It was a hub full of energy that brought people together and encouraged idea generation.

Could that have been done for half the price either further out or in a hot desk space? One hundred percent!

Was it a status grab to say, 'We are in central London; we must be a serious company'? You betcha!

Did they think that by having a more central location, potential companies and individuals would want to work with us more? Of course.

Did it happen? No.

From setting up my company, having a base outside London and no showroom at all, I saw no discernible difference between having these amazing premises or not.

Do I think if a client is unsure whether to contract us or not, the showroom could help close the deal? Sure. But that told me that my offering was not good enough somewhere else. If they are still on the fence, I need to address this immediately (in a much less costly way).

With the evolution of hot desk locations like WeWork, a small business can find locations at a fraction of the cost, across a location, to offer flexibility and resources to their staff. I once rented two residential flats in different locations across London and used them as a base for different departments based on where the business was coming from. Once the business dried up in that location, I did not renew the lease and moved to a new location. I was tied in for six months at a time for a fraction of the cost.

Warehousing is slightly different, but again, location is everything. Further out but on the right transport roads can save a chunk of money for the sake of fifteen minutes of further travel.

I work in a stock-heavy industry, and the amount of money tied up in both stock and warehouse space is intense. It is part and parcel of the service I offer, but we were extremely careful about both size and location. You can always ramp up if needed, with both temporary warehousing and office space. It is almost impossible to ramp down once you are tied in.

Take your time to really analyse what you need. It is one of the biggest decisions you will make.

A modern-day business involves much more working from home. Is this something you should embrace?

Due to COVID-19, there will never be a return to the office on the same level ever again. However, the work-from-home model in itself is not the solution either. Here are the pros and cons.

THE PROS OF WORKING FROM HOME

FLEXIBILITY

If you trust your staff, giving them the ability to adapt their hours around their life, commitments and family has proven that it works. You need to hire the right people that can be self-motivated, but if you get it right, this offering can be exponentially rewarding.

MODERN COMMUNICATION

With the evolution of technology and the development of apps such as Microsoft Teams and Zoom, being physically in the meeting room to discuss ideas and projects is no longer a necessity. More and more tenders that I have undertaken have been over these platforms. With the nervousness still here (at point of writing), it still gives you an opportunity to pitch and network.

FINANCIAL

The saving on expenses from travel, potentially on salaries when hiring (as they do not need to be based in a city and charge city pricing anymore) and so on can all have a positive effect on cash flow. If you get efficient on when and where your team does meet, it saves a lot of money. This was highlighted for us in 2020–2021 when we looked at our expenses for travel, international travel and entertainment. It really shocked me knowing the cumulative amount we actually spend on this sort of stuff.

THE CONS

The main negative I have definitely seen working from home is that you see a notable dilution of interaction, culture, ideas, alignment and goodwill.

I have bunched these together, as they are all interlinked.

Culture is almost impossible to create over Zoom. It is the in-person understanding that crafts it. It is not what you say but how you say it. It is how you act, how you interact with each person. It is how you listen. It is how you craft and develop each relationship. This cannot be seen on camera.

When you are working in a 'bubble', you naturally concentrate on yourself. There is less understanding and goodwill to help or adapt to other departments when things are changing or going wrong. It is not a bad thing as such; it is just a natural feature of 'what you do not see, you do not think about' over time.

Last, there is no replacement for the ability to bounce ideas off of each other in person. I definitely noticed a drop-off of people actively trying to 'improve' the business in lockdown. Yes, everyone was working hard. Yes, everyone probably had their own fears and worries about COVID-19 and family. But people were more than happy to accept the way it is as the norm and not push boundaries and evolve. This was a strength of ours pre-pandemic. It is now a lot more forced, as people have evolved.

WHAT I WISH I HAD KNOWN

→ The higher the overheads, the lower the profit.

→ Your overheads are always higher than you think with hidden costs, so budget for the worst-case scenario.

→ Flexibility is one of the best parts of a small business. Maximise this fact.

→ No one extreme is best. Balance is key. Become a hybrid.

→ Staying on top of the nuances lost to the pandemic is key as a CEO—culture especially.

→ Making sure your team is understanding and respectful at all times is important.

WHAT IS YOUR BIGGEST WASTE OF MONEY IN THE MODERN ERA?

Paid traditional advertising.

There is a reason TV advertising is struggling and newspaper revenue from adverts is on its knees. Radio and TV advertising works on a large scale when targeting a mass market. But putting a printed article in a local magazine or paper is such a waste of money, you might as well set fire right now to the wad of money in your wallet you are about to spend!

It is not up for negotiation. *Do not do it.*

There is a reason the three biggest companies for advertising in the modern era are Google, Facebook and Amazon. It is because they have fine-tuned their data on you, the consumer. So much so that, in Amazon's case, they almost know what you want before you do. There have been rumours of Amazon offering a delivery service where they send you items they think you need each month with a returns box, and you send back what you do not need. I know for a fact they would probably get 75 percent of my order right. (Damn, I hate being predictable.)

For a small business, every penny counts. If the business is struggling before this point, and you believe that putting an advert somewhere is the answer, there is a good chance that in a year's time you will be closing the doors.

With the invention of Sky or Amazon, do you actually watch the adverts or fast-forward past them? With Netflix, you are actually paying for no adverts as part of the amazing content!

Now I would class Amazon Prime TV and Sky as a necessity in my house, and I still do not watch the adverts. I barely watch any live TV anymore. Now imagine people reading a local paper or magazine linked to your industry. Do you honestly believe you have the copywriting skills to capture an audience that is reading something that is not even a priority to them? Not a chance. Do not waste your time or your money.

Furthermore, within reason, you can advertise anything on Google or Facebook. For anyone that has had social media in the past few years, think of the shit that has been pushed to you through targeted ads.

I have been targeted for everything from alcohol to holidays to IBS treatment. I do not (and did not) have IBS but happened to mention out loud to my wife that our dog had an issue with it. And just like that, through the wonders of the microphone on my iPhone, within sixty minutes and for two weeks, I was being pushed everything from online doctors to fibre to exercise to tablets to a special cushion to sit on should those problems worsen!

They have created an ecosystem where you can spend as little or as much as you want to target as many or as few people as you need. The fine-tuning is endless, and for many people it is the single biggest avenue for success selling a product.

Now, for me, this did not work, as I sell a hybrid product-service offering. Like I mentioned before, it works on a referral basis from a few key gatekeepers, so our resources were used to target in a slightly more old-fashioned way. I put my resources into LinkedIn rather than the more commercial advertisers.

Like gambling in Vegas, every pound spent in traditional advertising you must expect not to get back in any form, and *if* you win, it is a lucky bonus. They know their reader demographic about as well as you do.

Now, I am not going to pretend I have not done it, even though I am the biggest cynic out there. One particular sales member works in a niche industry that functions like something from the Stone Age, even though we work in a modern market. He half-heartedly argued that in order to increase our awareness in this area of the market, we had to follow what worked (I did not agree or believe) and that it would benefit in the long run (I never saw any justifiable return on this). But I backed him anyway, on a small scale, because it was important to him; I gave him a sales angle, and it cost very little. Sometimes the leap of faith in the person is more important than the lesson. The return on investment from the person for backing him was probably worth a lot more than the money spent on wasted advertising.

WHAT I WISH I HAD KNOWN

→   Do not waste your money.

→   Any person who sells traditional advertising and says they know who
    their reader demographic is is lying.

→   That money is better spent in almost any other area of the business.

PART V

STAFF

I have spent more time trying to understand my team, develop them and help them evolve than on any other aspect of the business. Staff can have such a lasting effect (both good and bad) on your business that you literally cannot put enough time and energy into them. It is also the hardest area to get right.

The next set of lessons highlights all the key areas I came across that either had the biggest impact or consumed the most time in driving the business forward.

BUILDING A TEAM

WHAT ARE YOU LOOKING FOR?

Provided you have your numbers right and the business makes financial sense, putting together a team is *the* single most important part of your business that can make or break it. Hiring the wrong person early on has far-reaching consequences and can bring down a company almost single-handedly. Hiring the right people can underwrite your business excellence and culture forever.

In an ideal scenario, you will have a gauge of some of the people who would 'suit' your business or have an area of specialty you need. Again, normally they are people within your industry that you have worked with or experienced on some level. Being a CEO and jumping into it boils down to making a few key decisions; the rest is gut instinct.

Being a judge of character or determining who is a good fit for your company falls into the 'gut instinct' category. You can know their work, their skillset and what they bring to the company, but it is a gut decision whether you think they will fit in and succeed in the new environment. I have always prided myself on being a good judge of people and finding their inner ability from a business perspective. (I still made a few errors along the way.) The lessons I learnt are noted below.

Ask yourself: What is it I am looking for? The principles I set out looking for were:

WORK ETHIC

I knew, above everything else, I wanted someone who was a grafter. Who was not afraid to contribute to departments that were not theirs if required and would go the extra mile. After all, a startup is hell for the first two years, so they had to be willing to do what was necessary. I have learnt that people either have this in them or they do not. No matter how much money you offer or the dream you sell them, this is not something you can train.

HONESTY, INTEGRITY AND TRUST

After my previous company and experiences, it was apparent that the lack of these things in a company is like a virus that courses through the veins of a business and is almost impossible to eradicate.

If your people are led by personal goals rather than the common goal, you will never be aligned. I could not be everywhere in the new setup, nor did I want to be, and this business was my baby, my pride and joy, everything that was good about me. I had to trust every person to look after it accordingly. This ability to make the right decision *in spite of* personal goals is a hard trait to find and an impossible trait to train.

BELIEF

You need someone that believes.

By this, I mean they need to believe in you, they need to believe in the 'mission' and they need to believe there is a future for them and they have made the right decision.

As mentioned previously, there are going to be some sticky spots along the way. There are going to be some hard decisions to be made and what feel like dark times. If the belief is not there, the business is susceptible to commitment falling by the wayside, people leaving or internal dissent. Belief, like hope, gives people drive in the face of adversity. It is on you, as the leader, to embolden them with this and help them believe. Once you do this, they will then do this for others, and the culture and belief will grow exponentially.

WHAT I WISH I HAD KNOWN

→ Take your time to hire the right people for the business. It is one of the most important decisions you will make.

→ Non-quantifiable traits are some of the most important.

→ If you can bring a team of excellent individuals together to run the company, you can then concentrate on driving it forward.

WORK ETHIC VERSUS TALENT

WHO WINS?

In every workplace, the most talented members of your company are praised, whether it is for their unique skillset, their adaptability under pressure or their natural gift at closing a deal. However, when it comes to a choice between the person with work ethic or the person with talent, the decision is easy.

I always pick work ethic every time, and I will explain why.

You cannot train someone in work ethic. I have tried and tried, but you just cannot. They either have it or they do not. They either want it or they do not. I have never met a person I have hired or worked with that had an average or worse work ethic at the beginning that changed and improved, that worked harder the longer they worked somewhere. Many times I have hired someone, knowing that their work ethic 'was not all that', but still hired them based on balancing all their pros and cons together. It is not a trainable skill. It is a mindset, and as a rule, I find that 99 percent of people do not change.

Look at your closest and longest friends from ten years ago to now. Have they fundamentally changed their predisposition that much? They may have lost a bit of weight, found God or changed a bit, but they are fundamentally the person now that they were then.

My ditzy, clever friend is still my ditzy, clever friend.

My so-laid-back-I-will-almost-fall-over friend? Still super chill.

My hard-working friend in his dream job, second-guessing whether he is good enough, so never letting off? You guessed it. Still the same: second-guessing and grafting harder than anyone in his industry.

The point is, a hard-working 'rough diamond' can, over time, be taught skills to become more efficient, to dress better and to learn the terminology or technical skills. But asking a person to hit the phones, knock on doors, or go that extra mile for a customer because sales is a numbers game based on volume of calls and quotes? You cannot train those skills.

In sport, how many players had the talent to be a star but let it go to waste? Every sport is littered with examples. Yet if you look for the best example, in football for instance, Cristiano Ronaldo, ever since he was starting out, worked harder than everyone else on the training field. The quotes are endless.

'For me, what stands out is the ability or the will to put in the effort *in every single minute of the game. Ronaldo's drive separates him from everyone else. Playing at the top level, everyone has talent, but I don't think anyone has the will that he has.'*

—VIRAT KOHLI, INDIAN CRICKET CAPTAIN

It is a story of legend that he was the first one on the training ground and the last one to leave, day in and day out.

Do not get me wrong; I am not saying turn your nose up at talent! But if you look at the best people in your industry, they will have a mix of both talent and work ethic, and I promise you the best people will always have work ethic right at the top of their skillset. Every company needs soldiers to be a success, and soldiers are built on an unwavering effort to succeed. Come hell or high water, they are in, 100 percent.

WHAT I WISH I HAD KNOWN

→ A person with talent *and* work ethic is a unicorn. Do not let them out of the building.

→ Small businesses need people willing to go the extra mile. People with work ethic have that in droves.

→ You can be successful in business just by outworking the competition in many scenarios when they are not at their best.

DO YOU LIKE MANAGING PEOPLE? DO YOU REALLY WANT TO?

Before I set up my business, I was a hungry salesperson. They called me Pac-Man (true story—as in the eighties computer game).

This was because of my speed at closing business—I sold every client the same package. I just went along gobbling up the easy deals. Back in the day, the package I sold was priced perfectly for many markets, I could duplicate my presentation, and in turn I could send out more quotes than anyone else. More quotes = more deals = more money.

However, at my previous company, deep down I always wanted to manage people. Managing people (in my mind) was a sign of experience; it was a sign of trust and also of progress.

It was also the next avenue to make more money. Have people work under you, take a cut of their earnings on top of your business and happy days! You are 20 percent better off year on year.

I could see no downside.

Like all people I started with one person—she was fantastic (she joined me at my new venture and still works with me and is still fantastic)—and then moved on to my second, and again it went well. The second person was a lot harder to manage, but the bit I prided myself on from a young age was being a 'people person': 'a person who enjoys or is particularly good at interacting with others'.

I was always a calm person, a good listener (personal opinion—I have zero data to back this up) and extremely positive—all traits I saw would make a good manager. Plus, above all else, I genuinely find most people extremely interesting. What made them tick made me tick and in turn drove us both.

After a few years, I progressed further to sales director, and my pitch for this role was based, above all else, on the fact that I was a people person and could get the best or better from them. I could bring the team together with more love and attention than they were getting. This all happened to be true, by the way. This was the bit I was the most excited about. I could not wait to make a difference.

But going from managing two people in a tight-knit unit to eventually managing fifteen is very, *very* different. Managing people is *not* what I thought it would be.

First off, never at any one stage is everyone happy. I would take 80 percent of my team being happy from one week to the next as the biggest win ever.

People are demanding. Demanding of your time, demanding of

your attention, demanding of your perceived opinion of them, demanding of your perceived opinion of them in regards to their colleagues.

Imagine your biggest personal fears as a person in business—jealousy, stress, home life problems, money problems, drug problems, missing sales figures, people stealing deals off you, age gaps, different stages of life, clashes of personalities in the office, pay rise demands. These were all weekly occurrences.

Add in the need for fifteen-plus different management styles to deal with all this, and it is beyond exhausting.

For every person you could put your arm around and give them a positive pep talk and the next week they would be flying, you had a person taking the piss and cruising along being lazy and going through the motions.

A firm talking-to with one person could get them motivated again. But to another, it could destroy the remaining spirit they had left and set them further down a negative path. It is exhausting even writing this down.

For every lead I gave to one person, another team member would be jealous or annoyed it did not go to them (even when the system was fair). There is no right way to deal with people because people's reactions are not always built out of logic; they are built out of emotion, their own insecurities and how something affects them.

This was by far the hardest part of the new role. It was truly exhausting, both emotionally and physically, to the point where the enjoyment of dealing with people was stripped completely. Once you take that management role within a business, you have to distance yourself completely from everyone. You can no longer be their friend, as you are their boss. The whole dynamic changes, and the camaraderie is lost.

So when I set up this new business, I was aware of the pitfalls. I was a few years wiser, definitely more mature and had even more standing internally, as it was my business.

The 'game changer' this time, though, was that these were 'my people'. All personally handpicked by me. People I had worked with before. All people where I knew what I was getting before they walked in the door. No surprises.

...and surprise, I was wrong again.

I am not going to pretend. It is a lot better having an existing relationship with these people, making the communication easier. But it is by far still the hardest part of the job and the part I enjoy the least, when once again I thought I would enjoy it the most.

If you accept that people are never actually happy and you cannot please everyone all the time, it makes the role so much easier. I have accepted that I cannot be everything to everyone, so I have chosen to be as honest, open and fair as possible with every employee. If that is not enough, at least then I can say I did my best and they know where they stand.

To actually try and keep everyone happy does the opposite. It keeps no one happy. I associate this with being the leader of a country who has to make decisions for all people. It is impossible to have everyone happy. The best you can do is put forward your manifesto for the way you want to lead the people forward. When the dust settles at the end, you can say you did what you thought was right. *PS: Do not start me on the current state of leadership around the world. Probably not the best example of decision-makers.*

The point of this chapter is to say that managing people is time-consuming. Every person who joins changes the dynamic. Every additional person involves a greater web of interaction between more people.

I remember when we had ten people, we had a system, a dynamic, and everyone knew where they stood. It felt like a startup. Everyone thrived on the fact that it was a startup and everyone was knee-deep in growing and learning on the fly.

A year later and at twenty people, we had so much friction across all areas. Fears of dilution of culture, favouritism, delegation of time and capacity. The list was endless. Growth was needed for the company to evolve and grow, but for six months it was tense. Everything had to be relearnt. At ten people, you did not need procedures; you just got on with it. At twenty people, everyone had to understand and learn.

I still love the people I work with, but I spend more time on the phone to my team on a daily basis than I speak to everyone external in the world in a week. Be prepared.

WHAT I WISH I HAD KNOWN

→ Managing people is about them taking and taking and you giving and giving. Do not expect this to be an equal transaction.

→ For every person you hire, the dynamic changes. Be prepared to adapt.

→ Try and grow your business with as few people as possible for an easier life.

WHY DOES EVERYONE THINK THEIR EXCUSES ARE SPECIAL? IT IS YOUR JOB TO SPOT THEM

'We have heard it all before' is a famous cliché for a reason. There is a big difference between constructive feedback and excuses.

Yet it never ceases to amaze me that people still come to me with these wild and wonderful reasons why they lost a deal, why they could not achieve something or hit a target. At the same time, it never ceases to amaze me even more that managers soak it up on face value time after time without constructive questioning. It is your job to decipher the difference.

It is your job as a business owner to be curious at a minimum and full-on detective if required. I want to caveat this extremely heavily. If you trust a member of your staff and they are generally consistent and reliable, you have no reason not to believe them. You should—they have earned it. In a small company, trust is both earned and a fundamental underpinning of the business.

However, especially in sales, but also in other departments, people manipulate the truth, exaggerate and frame excuses to protect themselves and direct the conversation in the way they want. This is extremely damaging to a business, as it can start to mask problems in regards to missing targets and relationships with staff members, even down to the culture of the whole company.

WHAT TO DO IN THESE SITUATIONS

1. LISTEN TO THE PERSON—OBVIOUSLY

After all, an unhappy or non-focused staff member is an asset that is not working for the company as best as they can. A lot of the time, a staff member just wants to be heard. Within that conversation, you can pick up a lot of other information that you would not get otherwise to craft a better picture. This is hugely beneficial in the future when dealing with that person again, as you will have a greater understanding.

2. KEEP A RECORD FOR YOURSELF

Your mind as a CEO is always working at 100 percent. You are never going to remember everything about everyone. Note down things in a personal file of a staff member so when the next incident occurs, you can track whether there are inconsistencies in the information.

3. ASK QUESTIONS

To merely accept what you hear at face value is negligence on your part to yourself, your business and other staff. You have a duty to ask questions. As mentioned above, an excuse is quite obvious to spot, but the reason and angle for it are not always so clear-cut. The more questions you ask and the more detail you get, the more will be revealed.

I know for a fact that the more people talk about their life or problems before a big meeting, the more likely it is that the information they are going to give me is going to be negative, whether it is a missed target or deadline. This is because they are trying to frame the conversation before it starts so you have pity for them, in the hope that you do not drive into the details with them from a professional point of view. Do not be fooled by it.

At my previous company, one salesperson built a web of intricate lies and emails that made it appear that a huge deal was in the pipeline. Every time the pressure got put on him and questions were asked, the deal was delayed, but only because the overall value of the deal got bigger! He knew nobody was going to be brave enough to pull him from a huge account that he was 'close to closing'. This also protected him from failing monthly sales figures, as he was 'concentrating' on a deal so big it would make the whole year a success. It took nine months and a lot of digging before his lies started to fall apart. That was when we found out the deal was dead six months earlier. It became a Ponzi scheme or shield for him to bide his time to replace this lost deal with other sales. It did not happen. He did not last much longer.

WHAT I WISH I HAD KNOWN

→   Empathy is so important, but excuses are dangerous.

→   Always trust a person if they have earned it.

→   Listening will tell you more than anything you ask.

THE HIRING FAILURE CONUNDRUM

THE IMPACT OF A SINGLE BAD HIRE

This was the advice I read before setting up my company: only hire the best. Whatever you do, make sure in the first five hires, you bring in the right people. If you do not, it can have a lasting impact on your business—to the point where it can result in closing the business.

Talk about scaring the hell out of me in making a hiring decision!

No one likes to admit that they were wrong. Hiring someone that does not work out has far-reaching consequences. Here are the main three:

ACCOUNTABILITY

First, *you* hired them. There is no hiding this fact, no diluting this fact. You are the boss, and only you are accountable for this. It really makes you take a long, hard look at yourself in the mirror and question your abilities when this happens. When you take it into your next hire and start second-guessing yourself, it can spiral into a pattern of bad hires.

FINANCIALLY

You feel you have wasted precious resources that were invaluable to a startup, sending it in the wrong direction. The guilt really makes it tough to accept that you have directly affected the business negatively. You realistically do not see a massive return on your investment of a hire in the first year, after salary and training. Most hires do not hit their stride for the first six months. You then really need to commit another six months to see if it is worth it. Before you know it, you have wasted £50,000 plus.

EMOTIONALLY

You personally hired that person. You probably gave them longer in the company than you should have. You may be seeing their 'potential', that future deal or project they were on the cusp of completing or winning. You then start questioning yourself and whether you are the problem. Could you have done more for that person? Is it your management at fault? Are you a bad judge of character? You want to believe that you could have done more and they are the right person but you are a bad teacher.

I made all of these mistakes. All were my fault. Below is a first-hand example. I am sharing my experience.

One of my early recruits came to join my new venture having

worked with me for years previously. They were reliable, with a solid character and existing client base. The basis for success. However, over the first year, their main client stopped delivering the business levels expected due to a change of direction. The employee went from working at a big organisation to working from home or satellite locations, and the cultural shift was too much. They were used to being man-managed more than I was aware, so the self-motivation was not there.

The first part was unfortunate but could be addressed.

As I had transferred from a big corporate environment to a small, niche, friendly environment, I assumed everyone else would adapt as well. Second, because they were experienced, I expected them to just slot right in and continue doing what they had done before. Why would they not? But there are so many intricacies to a startup or new business compared to an established entity, from obvious areas, such as procedures and systems, to less obvious ones, such as mindset. Going from the leader in an industry to the underdog is a huge mental reset. There is a swagger that comes when always pitching as the favourite with years of company reputation behind you. The second and third points were naivety on my part and hard lessons for me to learn.

Every single employee you hire has a massive impact on the success or failure of your business. Unlike big businesses, who can carry mediocre employees and have their average contribution help, *you cannot.*

As a small company, you want rock stars and heroes. Employees whose contributions both monetarily and culturally far outweigh their cost. Salary is one of your biggest costs as a growing small business. You want to maximise the return on it; otherwise, it is just a waste.

WHAT I WISH I HAD KNOWN

→ Hiring is so difficult. Even sure things sometimes do not work out.

→ Do not underestimate the cultural aspect of the job change.

→ Have you done enough to make this person a success?

THE GOLDEN RULES FOR LETTING A PERSON GO AT A SMALL BUSINESS

Everyone in a management role, at some point, has fired someone. This is the hardest part of the job. It comes with the territory as a business owner. Even the greatest companies in the world do not have a 100 percent successful record of recruitment. This is because there are so many variables that can impact that person's success.

Sacking someone as a fellow employee is tough, even if you hired them. But you have the ability to take the big-company angle of 'it is part of a restructure', 'the fit was not right' or 'we are going in a different direction' (literally all the cliché breakup lines for relationships but tailored for work). But when it is your business, it stings. I mean, it really stings! This is because you have no shield. It is your decision, 100 percent.

How a company deals with redundancies of staff has far-reaching consequences to both that person and the existing staff afterwards. The amount of companies that get this wrong by taking the easy way out is much higher than it should be.

To minimise all the negative effects that can be associated with this tough part of business management, I have listed all the key points you need to consider.

1. IT IS YOUR FAULT

- You must accept immediately that any person you let go in your business because they 'have not worked out', were not the 'right fit' or were generally outright rubbish is completely your fault. I have talked about this before regarding hiring, but it is equally important at the other end of the employment cycle.
- Whether you hired them or not, it is your fault.
- If they lied on their CV or the market changed, it is your fault.

For as long as hiring is one of the most important parts of running a small business (see previous lesson) and your name is above the door, so to speak, and you own it, it is on you.

Once you accept this, you will view every person you hire differently.

- You will improve your recruitment technique.
- You will improve how you perceive people.
- You will put more effort into your in-house training.
- You will spend more time with them.

This is because *hiring* and *firing* is the biggest ball ache out there!

Once you have let your first person go, you will never look at recruitment the same again.

The list of negatives of an unsuccessful hire are many. Here are the key ones:

- They consume time (yours and many others').
- They consume short-term and long-term financial costs (salary, commission, even recruiter fees).
- They affect morale on the way in and the way out. The current team think they are under pressure on the way in, and then feel that they are potentially expendable on the way out if you are seen to sack people they perceive as good enough to stay.
- It can be a legal minefield.

Even if you do everything right and manage them out and tick every rule of the book, there is always the potential of them feeling unfairly dismissed or discriminated against.

That is their prerogative.

I have never had this happen at my company, but it is worth consideration. HR friends of mine have also shared some of the disputed dismissal reasons. Even if there are no grounds for dispute, it still consumes time, stress and potentially finances.

2. IT IS PERSONAL

- There is a big difference between a big company and a small company when it comes to hiring and firing. Big companies recruit people to their firm based on their reputation and offering. Small companies recruit on faith in the owner and the dream.
- Big companies make redundancies. Small companies let people go.
- It is personal. Let us make no mistake; when it comes to letting someone go, as much as it is a business decision and they may have been useless, it is personal to them!

Letting someone go is like ending a relationship. The longer it has gone on, the more each party has vested in the other. What you tell them can have a long-term impact on their self-esteem and own perception. Think of the relationships you had when you were younger, when you knew deep down it was not working out, but your girlfriend or boyfriend at the time started being distant. It is the worst feeling. Then when they did split up with you, the reasons they gave were absolute bullshit. 'It is not you; it is me', 'I am not in the right place right now', 'You deserve better' or 'I cannot offer you what you want'. All utter crap!

Looking back, how much would you have preferred someone just to say to you, 'I just do not fancy you enough'? Yes, it would have stung at that moment, but you would have known exactly where you stood and could move on.

The corporate world does this more than you think. Managers blame the finances or the company fit or a change in direction. None of those are constructive. Letting one person go and then blaming it on the finances of the business is beyond insulting.

Either you are in a bad position, so you need to let a lot of people go, or it is an excuse. I have never known a situation where saving £2,000 to £3,000 a month meant the business would survive or not.

3. BE HONEST

- Be as honest as you can be without being cruel. If you have spent time with your staff over a period of time, giving feedback on a timely basis (which, in a small team, is essential, as you are involved in most things), then as long have you have been consistent with them, anything you tell them at the point you fire them should not be a complete shock.
- In sales, numbers are expected. They are not everything, but there is an expectation on team members to deliver results. This is very quantifiable.
- In creative industries that are not easily black and white, setting a set of expectations in other areas is very important.

THE RULES

I have experienced three separate examples of letting people go that had to be managed carefully. In all those scenarios, I abided by three golden rules.

1. KEEP IT SHORT AND KEEP IT PRECISE

- When I let them go, it was hard. In some cases, they were friends (and still are). Short-term, it affected our friendship, but long-term, it was beneficial.
- It is not a discussion; it is a decision. Nothing they can say will change your mind.
- They are adults, so treat them like they are.

In a small business there is no room to carry people, which is an ethos you should communicate to everyone from when you set up the business. This sets a clear understanding for success.

2. MAKE IT A CLEAN BREAK

- Let them go immediately. For both the person you are letting go and the staff still remaining, ripping the plaster off helps after the initial shock. It stops misunderstanding, embarrassment, and denting of pride and protects culture.

3. MAKE THEM A GOOD LEAVER

- Pay them more than they are owed (sometimes more than they deserve). This buys goodwill and a more positive long-term impact. Should they talk about the company, this will be their final memory of you.

THE REAL-WORLD EXAMPLE: THE FLATTERING CV

I include this because it is a firsthand example that taught me two very different lessons.

1. CVs are a minefield.

2. No amount of asking questions beats knowing someone who has worked with or knows of that person. Real-world application and experience cannot be beaten.

Being a small company, you should recruit only from word of mouth until you are looking for operators rather than innovators. Not until you have exhausted every avenue internally should you ever look externally. Recommendations in every area of a small business are priceless, and recruitment is no different. The risks and unknowns of using a recruiter or, in this case, being approached are much higher than the risks of someone being put forward.

In my case, I was approached on LinkedIn and our business Instagram page by a person looking for a job. They sent a great email with a comprehensive breakdown of why they were looking for a job (good sales pitch) and why our company would suit them and they would suit us (flattery—again, good sales). The company they had worked for had closed (valid reason), and they were being proactive looking for work. It ticked all the boxes.

Now, as I did not know them, the recruitment process was much more thorough and spread across three separate interviews with three senior people. Three people who I trust in the company. Three people I recruited. Three people who understand the culture of our business better than anyone else.

All three of them gave a unanimous yes. The potential hire was dynamic and blew us away with their CV and talk. Their CV was comprehensive, with a history of success, if spread across a number of companies. (They attributed changing jobs to ambition. *In hindsight, this should have been a red flag, but it was brushed over.*)

They seemed like an ideal fit. The only thing that was not entirely the truth on their CV was the number of jobs they had previously. After all that, it was a disaster. All that hard work was a myth.

I had access to their diary, and I think over their life cycle I probably paid them £1,000 per meeting booked. They did so little! Once they had exhausted their black book of contacts initially, there was no get up and go. They would come to every sales meeting and tell a fantastic story about what was coming and who they had networked with. I just had to wait a bit longer. They did just enough to make me believe there was hope. And I soaked it all up for longer than I care to admit.

Every warning sign was there, but I still persevered for all the reasons I have spoken of recently: faith, belief, not accepting I had recruited badly, not accepting I had done something wrong. When I finally let them go, I had probably wasted £20,000 in salary and commission (about six months' worth). And you know what? Eighteen months later, we are still sorting through the problems that they left.

Nothing I saw from the interview process was there. After about week three, I knew what I had on my hands but did nothing. Sometimes, as harsh as it is, it is okay to make a swift and definitive decision. Nine months later, they were exactly the same. Worse, even. Only then, after a lot of influence from my senior management team, did I make the move and let them go.

Looking back, I was not only foolish; I was naive. I wasted, proportionally, a fuck ton of money that could have been better used elsewhere. It was all my fault from start to finish—truthfully, 100 percent on me.

When it came to letting them go, there was no pushback. In fact, I think they were a bit shocked they had lasted this long collecting a pay cheque. As frustrated as I was (at both myself and them), I still followed my rules: immediately cut off, a good leaver, and a compensation package probably larger than it should have been. I believe in goodwill in all scenarios.

WHAT I WISH I HAD KNOWN

→ Once all assessments are done, make decisions swiftly.

→ Be honest with feedback.

→ A clean break always.

PART VI

A YEAR IN REVIEW

And that is it. Three hundred sixty-five days of absolute slog. Three hundred sixty-five days of blood, sweat, and tears. There were all of them at some point. I can truly say I was broken. Physically burnt out, mentally exhausted and emotionally fragile. You are likely to experience something similar.

Was it worth it? Without a shadow of a doubt. Would I do it again? Show me where to sign up!

The end of the year for a business is like New Year's Day for the normal person. It is a chance to take stock of the past year, forgive yourself for eating too much food and drinking too much alcohol at Christmas and start afresh.

Take some quiet time to review the year. The highs, the lows, the wins, the fails. Soak it up and reset. Very rarely will you get a chance to just digest. Make sure you do. It is priceless.

SO HOW DID I GET ON?

Here are my key takeaways from my first year:

1. I spent more than I made in profit. I invested in ten people. I fast-tracked my year two projections into year one with a small amount of external funding to get it up to speed as quickly as possible. Upon review of the year, the £250,000 invested has gone on a new warehouse, a lot of stock, two vans, two different brochures, a website, and 'buying some wins'—lower-margin sales to get a foot in the door.
2. My sales were higher than expected (win) but the margin contribution made was much lower (loss).
3. Technically, as a business, we recorded a £200,000 loss!
4. Cash in the bank was tight, and we just about covered ourselves on a monthly basis.
5. Hidden costs are a killer on a business. Many tiny costs really start to chip away and add up to a big cost. I need to assess our margin and how to rein in these costs.
6. The service we have brought to the market is by far the best.

Bring on year two!

WHAT I WISH I HAD KNOWN

→ This is much harder than I thought.

→ The government really makes it as hard as possible for a business to be a success (different versions of taxes).

→ I was more naive to setting up and running a business than I thought I would be. Learning on the job is an understatement. But it is the best learning curve.

→ I could not have done it without my business partner. My appreciation levels for him are not quantifiable. I have lucked out in having someone opposite of me in every way. We bring out the best in each other and get stronger every month.

PART VII

THE MIDDLE

By now I was 'established' as a business in the marketplace.

By this I mean I had a functioning, working business, with staff, premises, a team and regular business. A good guide that you are doing something right is that sales are going up but also that competitors have taken notice and started talking shit about you. We must be doing something right.

The lessons learnt from this stage on are very different from the earlier pages of the book. They are equally important to your next phase of growth. You may have set strong foundations and the basis for something great. But if you do not develop from here and get better at every opportunity, then you are still at risk of failure.

Here is what I wish I had known.

IF YOU ARE NOT ASSESSING, YOU ARE GUESSING

What is your judgment of success? What is your understanding of a product or service that fills a need? How do you gauge feedback?

The amount of people I have spoken to that 'know' that their customer is happy or that their product is a 'success' is ridiculous. Everyone makes sweeping assessments from feelings or judgment calls. They make these with no real substantive data, and this is beyond dangerous for a small business.

If you can answer any of these questions, then I trust you, and your judgment is where it should be. Anything less and it is time to reassess.

1. Has your customer left you a review on a public forum? (See next lesson.) People really only leave reviews if they either love or hate a product or service they have received.

I know I do. Anything in between and they are indifferent to making the effort to pass feedback.

2. Have you called and spoken to the end user for honest feedback? If you have not, how important is that client to you, really? Especially at the beginning!

3. Have they ordered more than once? Loyalty and repeat business are king for a small business.

4. Are you getting organic growth without advertising? This normally means word of mouth is helping you grow. This is sometimes hard to tell, but your revenue and turnover figures are a good gauge. Word-of-mouth growth is a staple of the small business and, as discussed before, something that should be leveraged as much as humanly possible.

In my experience, I really pushed on all these areas.

In year one, whilst it was still realistic, I called as many customers and introducers as physically possible. This was to either check in or thank them for placing their orders. Other than the value of my time, I saw no negatives to doing this. And boy, did I learn a lot I would not have otherwise—concerns about initial quality, delivery service, all the way down to how my staff were dressed. It was priceless.

WHAT I WISH I HAD KNOWN

→ You have to be getting true, consistent feedback on your product or service.

→ Thinking you know how well you are doing is a fast track to failure.

→ Make sure sales are increasing. This is a great gauge. Once the sales are in place, you can start to fine-tune the profit you make.

THE IMPORTANCE OF EXTERNAL RECOGNITION

REVIEWS AND AWARDS

Eventually, you need a trusted forum for review. Not every user can be bothered to give feedback, but pressing as many people as possible associated with every deal is so important. It eventually becomes an extension of our sales pitch.

The only time this does not necessarily apply is for very high-end luxury goods, as people want the exclusivity of ownership without necessarily publicising it.

When you buy a product or check out a restaurant in the twenty-first century, how much of your decision is based on a review? I bet it is more than you think. Whether it is Trustpilot, Google or Tripadvisor, you need to believe that what you are buying, using or eating is going to be as you expect.

When it comes to your company, this expectation from customers is no different.

When starting up, you have no reputation, no track record, and you are looking for a leap of faith from the buyer. A word-of-mouth recommendation from a friend will convince the prospective customer to use you. This is a version of an award or recognition early on.

However, at a certain stage you become about more than paying the bills. You become about building a legitimate company. The word-of-mouth referral becomes limited in its marketing ability. It is, at times, detrimental, as the perception is you are still a small company.

An award is a concrete, fly the flag at full mast, shout it from the rooftops recommendation that you are trustworthy, real and, above all, 'the best at what you do'. Even if not all of that is completely true, perception is everything. People love a winner!

How many times have you seen the words 'from Academy Award–winning director', 'six-time Emmy-nominated' or 'six-time Champions League winner'? (Yes, I am a Liverpool fan.)

How many times have you chosen not to eat at a restaurant or get takeaway you loved because the hygiene rating was three out of five? I know I have!

The point is that stuff like this can make or break a business. Once you have established the foundations of your business, this is a vital next step to help drive the business forward.

As I have mentioned before, a successful business is not built on a foundation of one magic pill or offering. It is built on a cumulative improvement across all areas of the business, so when all added together, they offer something that is the best.

A review is a consistent, trusted and easily found way to show every future customer that you are what you say. That you are all the things listed above:

Reputable ✓

Reliable ✓

Real, even! ✓

Then on top of this, by association, great at what you do ✓

Five stars literally tells you this.

The fact that someone has taken the time to write a review shows they are willing, in a public forum, to back you. This is better than any paid marketing. It should be something you roll out as soon as you can.

PS: There is an award for anything if you look hard enough. Get that recognition!

WHAT I WISH I HAD KNOWN

→ Reviews and awards give you real-world recognition.

→ Reviews are a selling tool that you can highlight to help close deals without feeling like you are selling.

→ People want to associate with winners.

THE NEXT STAGE AS A CEO

The role of a CEO evolves over time.

As mentioned before, in Lesson 14, at the start, you are Mr or Ms Everything. Your job is to fundamentally keep the business alive; beg, steal and borrow orders and convince clients to use you; sell your soul to the devil; and drive the business forward by all means and sacrifices necessary. But what happens once you have passed that initial stage? What is your role?

If you have done the basics right and you have a functioning business that is generating income and clients, your role will naturally change. And it is important that you embrace and accept this.

Your role then becomes about bringing the different aspects and people of the business together to excel in what they do.

Your job, in a nutshell, is to deal with the crap. To allow your amazing staff to do what they do best, whether it is sales, marketing, operations or design. If you trust in the people you have hired, you want them to spend as much of their time as possible doing what they were brought in to do. Every hour they are involved in politics, non-essential admin or work that does not benefit or use them is a waste of a resource.

That resource is precious. This feels counter-intuitive to everything I have spoken about previously about running a business. It is even harder to put into place years down the line when you have been in the trenches on every minor decision.

Do not get me wrong; this is tough to do. The goal is to find a balance between the needs of the business, with its day-to-day running, and planning the future. But the more time *you* dedicate to being the problem-solver to as many of their needs or issues as possible, the more *they* can drive your business forward. You are supporting and enabling your staff.

If you have an amazing salesperson who is bringing in the money, why on earth would you let them get involved in a decision about the business unless it directly impacted their income? If they have ideas to make their job easier (which I would hope they would, if they buy into the company), then great. If they are constantly being drawn into administrative issues regarding shipping, stock or marketing, you are not doing your job.

You are the goalkeeper, the parent, the puppet master behind the curtain. Your job is to make them tick. Solve the admin task; help solve the shipping issue; network their introducers. Do whatever it takes to keep them concentrated on doing what they do best and what you need them to do.

We once had a delivery very early on to a place in central London for a client. We did not have the logistical capabilities we have now, and fundamentally, we were double-booked. We needed the team to do two jobs in one day in two different locations. They were both for founding clients (*clients we describe as people who took a chance on us right away without a track record—so very important*) who both had deadlines. Both deliveries did not even fit on one van, and three items we could not even get due to delays.

Your job as CEO is to solve that problem. It is as simple as that. The company has a pinch point that can affect it short-term? Then find a solution.

The answer in this case was to drive at 9:00 p.m. and collect all the smaller items from our warehouse. (It is a bold statement calling it a warehouse; at this point, it was more like a storage lock-up.) This was seventy miles in the opposite direction from the delivery address. Some of the items were too heavy for one person, so I roped in my brother to help for beer money. We then drove to delivery A, which had a twenty-four-hour concierge, and unloaded and unpacked all items, placing them in the right location. It was boring work and boiling hot in the apartment.

By doing this, when the delivery team arrived the next morning, I had saved them an hour unloading and an hour unpacking the smaller items. They also did not have to think about product locations, as they were already laid out. It was a small help, but it made a difference. That is all that mattered.

The next morning, whilst they were doing the technical stuff, I waited for the shops to open and bought the remaining missing items at retail cost, delivered them to the delivery address and managed to finish the offering we promised whilst saving the team enough time to go on to the next important delivery.

We made no money on the retail items. But by finishing both those jobs and saving our reputation before we began, I estimate it made us £400,000 in future orders over the next five years from those two customers.

They did not know we were renting a temporary storage lock-up. They did not know we had double-booked them with just one delivery team. They did not know I was at the delivery address until 1:00 a.m. unpacking and crushing cardboard boxes. They did not know that we had not fully sorted our stock system and did not have the items we promised. All they remember is that we delivered what we said we would and that we were reliable.

I still have photos of that installation saved on my phone. It means a lot! It is not pretty, and it is not glamorous, but have I not been saying all along that is the whole business ownership gig?

WHAT I WISH I HAD KNOWN

→ You are the parent to your wonderfully talented children. Your job is to keep them on the straight and narrow, doing what they are good at. If you keep their time free, they will deliver what they are good at.

→ There is no problem as a CEO that is too small.

→ Small differences can have a big long-term impact.

SALES

THE NUMBERS DO NOT LIE

'You are what your record is.'

—BILL PARCELLS

Bill Parcells, one of the most famous American football coaches of all time, used this line when an interviewer asked whether his team was unlucky and the record for them unfairly represented how good they really were and whether, with a bit of luck either way, his record could be completely different.

Now, most coaches or leaders who are under pressure would use this open invitation to lead the narrative down this road of luck in order to buy themselves some more time and help people see it from their point of view. But Bill called it for what it is.

I have learnt the hard way so many times, with salespeople at my previous employers and being a business owner, to take into consideration all of the other 'fluff'. Stuff like outside influences, personal issues, percentage of deals lost, the current state of the market, bad luck, how hard someone has been perceived to be working and how much value they add elsewhere. I also want to highlight that all these things have an impact and need to be taken into consideration.

But not as much as you think. And I promise you, I have heard them *all*. The numbers do not lie. Say it with me. The numbers do not lie. One more time...THE NUMBERS DO NOT LIE!

Salespeople have bad months. We all do, in any industry. But it is one of the few departments that can give you data that you can actually look at, analyse and track over days, weeks, months and years. And you are going to ignore it?!

If a salesperson is, on average, doing twenty sales a month, then why would you, for any reason, believe that they are suddenly going to jump to thirty?

Salespeople love to manipulate and tell their story, and sell their hype—*see my CV story in Lesson 32*. It is what we do. I should know because I was in sales for years. I could sell you the dream in minutes that would bring you to tears for a sale. But you need to see through it. When hiring someone, do not hope once they are a year or two into their tenure that they will do more sales or different business development than they are already doing...they will not. As a leader, it is negligent to think otherwise.

Every year I ask my sales team, based on their sales pipeline (what they have coming up) and introducers, to give me their predicted revenue targets for the year. The team then has a month to go away in March and present to me what they expect it to be. This will be a mix of 'guaranteed' orders, highly likely stuff based on their hard work in previous years, and then a reactive percentage on top of that.

I then look at their previous history of sales and make a prediction myself. Without fail, I am 25 to 30 percent closer than they are.

I know which salespeople like to sandbag (undervalue) their target so they appear to overachieve. I know which salespeople are slightly insecure (not a bad thing, by the way—this is a massive driver for lots of salespeople to prove themselves) and like to big themselves up and pick a number that is way too high.

You need to learn these types of things as well, and you will, with experience.

Why is this sales number important?

1. BUDGET PREDICTION

If your spend on stock is based on their predicted sales numbers and you are 30 percent short or 30 percent long, your cash flow is not being used efficiently. If you are running a small business like me, that could mean stock that you can later not get rid of and has to be sold at a discount. Or worse, you have not bought enough and so cannot maximise the potential sales you have.

2. CASH FLOW

Cash flow gives you options. It is also protection from the unknown. In the first couple of years, money is tight. I mean seriously tight. I mean not-paying-yourself-in-certain-months tight. If you overspend based on future expectations, this can leave you in a very precarious predicament if not accurate.

WHAT I WISH I HAD KNOWN

→ Sales is an area you can assess with accuracy. Make use of the data.

→ Be wary of the over-promiser. If you do not know them well, you may come unstuck.

→ Budgeting helps every single area of the business. Public companies are so good at it because they do not want to spook investors. Try and get yours as accurate as possible.

THE TEN-YEAR RELATIONSHIP

THE IMPORTANCE OF PLAYING
THE LONG GAME

Everyone is looking for business right now. Everyone is looking to make a quick buck and maximise the here and now.

It makes sense. We all have targets and money to earn and people who we are accountable to. However, if you look at where the deals are actually won, it is rarely at that moment. It is a process over months and years to align yourself with that decision-maker or company.

So when you lose a deal even though your product or offering is the best, you get upset. But in many cases, it was not yours to win. Barack Obama famously said, 'It took me ten years to become an overnight success'.

The role of a CEO is to train your team to think short-, mid- and long-term if they want to be a continued success. Training them appropriately will help your business grow long-term.

THE TEN-YEAR RELATIONSHIP EXAMPLE

Over a decade ago, someone I knew through a friend worked at a single-office business local to me. I was young and touting for business back then, crudely and without prejudice, to anyone that gave me a sniff of a deal. We started talking over mutual people we knew and where we lived. Now, subconsciously, I knew he was dynamic, and actually, I just liked him as a person. But where he worked was a waste of time and effort. His small, local area business model did not require what we offered, and it would involve selling someone something they did not need. At the time I was not above this, but it was just a lot of hard work for little reward.

I kept in touch, and we became 'work friends'.

'The way in which you interact at work leads people to believe you are best friends when in reality you would never have been seen outside work with them.'

—URBAN DICTIONARY

He was very private, and we talked generally but never managed to do any work together. I do not think he fully understood what I did (or at least did not see the value in it). Anyway, I kept in touch from time to time. After all, business is done in the times people do not have any business to offer you.

About two years later, I saw on LinkedIn that he had taken a bigger job in London for a company I was already dealing with. My first reaction was 'Result!' This makes my existing client a lot easier to deal with and can only benefit me now.

Fast-forward another two years. Due to the time frames of his projects, even though he was willing to work with me and give me business, he did not actually have anything for me. So doing the 'salesperson' thing, I kept in touch, popped in for coffees and so on. I did everything I needed to reap the rewards.

Just as we were three months out from being about to do proper business together...he decided to leave due to a management reshuffle and not liking his new boss. What are the chances?!

But, being the *great friend* that I was, I helped him get a job with one of my other clients. Win for him, but obviously a win for me again (so I thought). So here he is, indebted to me for helping him get out of a situation at his current job, into a promotion at a better company, and guess what? His new projects are another two to three years away. Unbelievable!

To keep the story shorter, he again changed jobs for another promotion to an even better company (as he is dynamic and great at his job, as mentioned previously). The next company's project pipeline? *Four* years from inception.

Anyway, the very belated point I was here to make is that he is now in charge of one of the flagship projects in London for the next ten years. He is in control of his destiny, loves what he does and is doing really well.

I am, of course, his preferred supplier, and we currently are generating more business from him than if I had combined all his previous roles. He is now and will continue to be one of the leading revenue generators.

The numbers on this relationship:

→ Total time committed to this person: Twelve years currently and counting...

→ Total number of coffees: Two hundred plus

→ Total number of lunches: Fifty plus

→ Number of events attended: Twelve to fourteen

→ Revenue to be generated over the next three years: £3,000,000

→ Number of companies he has worked for: Four

→ Number of companies I have worked for: Two

Did I know he was going to be a success? God, no. He was working in a small local business at the time.

Did I think he was too good for the job he was in? One hundred percent.

But this does not mean it had any potential benefit to me.

Did I at times wonder whether to cut my losses and stop wasting my time? Many, *many* times.

The point is you need to look at potential in every situation. Every sales clerk or administrator now could, in three to five years, be either somewhere else or in a more senior position that could benefit you. That sounds cold, but you are both in business together to be successful and prosper.

To quote Gordon Gekko in *Wall Street,* 'Now what's worth doing, is worth doing for money...it's a bad bargain if nobody gains'.

A small business owner does not have the luxury to let opportunity pass them by. The number of chances when starting up is tough when your company is based on work ethic, word of mouth and reputation. A relationship now could have an exponentially greater impact on your business in years to come.

WHAT I WISH I HAD KNOWN

→ A deal is not always done now, but the groundwork is.

→ Potential comes in many forms, and there is no time frame on this.

→ Do not underestimate lower-level positions. You were there once, and look at you now.

LESSONS I HOPE YOU DO NOT HAVE TO LEARN THE HARD WAY

1. BUSINESS IS HARD

It sounds obvious, does it not?

But it cannot be overstated.

Business is fucking hard. It takes and takes and takes, and just when you think you are getting a handle on it, it throws a spanner in the works. This is a constant. It continues to happen throughout your business journey. There is no cure for it, there is no answer to why it happens, but I promise it will get you at the worst time. All that you are left with is to work out how you are going to deal with it. In the end, that and the consequences that go with it are all that matters.

2. PEOPLE DO NOT CHANGE

As mentioned in Lessons 27 and 28, this is such an important lesson to learn. Deep down, when you look back on your life and the people you meet, it really does stare you in the face, and you will not believe you missed it.

Very few people change who they are by any significant amount. Use that to your advantage, as you know where you stand.[8]

This is so important in regards to work. Whilst training and management play a big part in developing a member of staff, and your culture and communication style may aid their work, let us not kid ourselves. You know who the superstars are in your division, in your company and in your industry. There are certain traits you can train and develop but also certain traits you cannot (as mentioned previously).

When setting up my company, I knew I had to hire as many superstars as possible. So I went for the best where feasible and financially possible. I then went for accountable, reliable, loyal, compassionate and hard-working. After that, everything else is insignificant.

I can tell you for a fact, you guessed it...my superstar is even more of a superstar, so damn good, in fact, that the company helped develop them even further into a fucking force of nature that no one wins against. Do not get me wrong; there are ele-

---

8   Tracy Brower, 'Research Says People Can't Change: How to Avoid Hiring Difficult People through Successful Selection', Forbes, November 3, 2019, https://www.forbes.com/sites/tracybrower/2019/11/03/research-says-people-cant-change-how-to-avoid-jerks-through-successful-selection/?sh=73dd4698a780; Cornelis B. Bakker, 'Why People Don't Change', *Psychotherapy: Theory, Research & Practice* 12, no. 2 (1975): 164–72, https://psycnet.apa.org/record/1977-08597-001?doi=1.

ments to them that are rough around the edges and areas that require nurturing and development. But fuck me, in the role they are in, from a business perspective, they kick arse and take names on a daily, weekly and monthly basis. No amount of training or development could get my tier-two employees to that level. You just have to weigh up the compromises!

On the opposite end of the spectrum is the staff member I worried deep down was a bit lazy. But I thought I could drive them forward. You guessed it. Yep, they are still lazy and, in fact, more so in a laid-back, less man-management environment. When I look back, it was me who was looking for something more positive than was actually there. When I let them go, all the things I was worried about deep down were still there.

3. EXPECT THE UNEXPECTED

If you do more things right than wrong, your company will progress on a certain trajectory in a positive direction. However, how you get there is never, *ever* smooth. Every time you think you have mastered something, another part will go wrong. As soon as you think one area is going to go really well, watch it fall apart whilst countering that a lost cause comes good. This has happened so many times in regards to sales and projected business that it is an in-house joke. Chaos theory at its best.

Chaos theory is defined as 'the study of apparently random or unpredictable behaviour in systems governed by deterministic laws'.[9]

---

9   Encyclopaedia Britannica Online, s.v. 'Chaos Theory', accessed June 6, 2022, https://www.
     britannica.com/science/chaos-theory.

Let me give you an example of this. Over the summer one year, all the data was projecting we would have a fantastic three months. But suddenly, projects got delayed, clients lost their jobs, and deals that were guaranteed were cancelled for the strangest reasons. One of the worst financial quarters on record!

Six months later, I was panicking about cash flow, as our pipeline looked empty only three weeks into the future. Then, almost overnight, we were maxed out for a month, beyond being able to deal with capacity and with not enough stock.

All you can do in those scenarios is embrace them, address them immediately, and make swift decisions to try and make the best of it.

4. LEARN THE GOLDEN RULE OF A CRISIS

'Bad companies are destroyed by a crisis, good companies survive a crisis, but great companies are defined by a crisis.'

—ANDY GROVE, CEO OF INTEL

This lesson naturally follows number three, expect the unexpected. The wonderful thing about this statement is, it is universal in its application to companies of all sizes. Whether you are Amazon or a one-man band, the collateral effects of a crisis are without judgment or favouritism. You can both be equally affected.

What is wonderful about a crisis is that it stresses every element of your business and tests its strengths and weaknesses. Most staff members work hard during the easy times. Put them under pressure in a stressful situation and you will see who they really are. How they communicate, how they interact, how they present themselves.

No company is perfect, but a crisis will really bring to the front its strengths and weaknesses for all to see.

We have all experienced probably the biggest crisis any business in the civilised Western world will ever deal with (excluding wars) in regards to COVID-19. Just look at the fundamental and irreversible impact it has had on so many industries. Everything we did before has changed on some level.

Look at the death of retail stores. Stores like Topman—which I would class as one of the kings of the high street. Names you would never have thought could go under and were a staple of the high-street shopper.

Almost overnight, COVID-19 highlighted their inability to evolve to online trade. So they have gone the way of the dodo. The biggest 'fuck you' was the purchase of Topshop by ASOS. This was the final nail in the coffin, so to speak, establishing that a new king of the jungle was here. ASOS is the online upstart that, when launched, no one believed would succeed. Conventional wisdom thought clothes could not be sold online due to sizing and people wanting to try them on. Now ASOS is buying the leader of the nineties and noughties, Topshop.

5. STAFF ARE THE HARDEST PART OF THE BUSINESS

I have touched on this in a previous lesson, but there is a direct correlation between more staff and more drama. It is not an equal equation and never will be. You have to give more than you get back. It is super tiring.

WHAT I WISH I HAD KNOWN

→ If you keep motivated and keep trying, day in and day out, your business will have a higher chance of being a success.

→ Expected the unexpected. It happens more than you would think.

→ Staff are a full-time job. Be prepared.

→ There will be no better time to judge the material strength of your business than under huge amounts of pressure.

→ If your business is strong and not in an industry directly affected by a shutdown, you may be able to thrive and take market share.

→ The ability of small companies to adapt quickly is priceless.

RELATIONSHIPS WIN DEALS— WHAT DOES THIS MEAN FOR YOUR BUSINESS?

'Business happens over years and years. Value is measured in the total upside of a business relationship, not by how much you squeezed out in any one deal.'

—MARK CUBAN

In Lesson 5, about trusting your gut instinct, I share a story to raise the point about not having a relationship with my customer, which lost me the deal. This has led me to discuss further the key highlights of that point.

'Do not kid yourself that your work is better—relationships win deals!' This was a backhanded dismissal I received over ten years ago. I lost a deal, and this particular person was the decision-maker. I applied pressure for constructive feedback (as you always should so you can learn from your mistakes).

After a relentless level of bombardment on my part, he eventually opened up and told the truth. He fundamentally said, 'I have given the deal to someone I know / like / am friends with more than you'.

From that moment, I have never lost a deal that I deep down knew I was going to win before I went into a pitch—a true story, I promise. It is like having a loaded deck of cards.

Sun Tzu had a famous saying: *'Every battle is won or lost before it is ever fought'*. Talk about a high-brow reference. Bet you did not think you would be getting philosophical musings in this book, did you? Neither did I, to be fair!

But when it comes to business, it is gospel.

I estimate that when I am pitching purely based on the quality of my work, I win approximately 20 percent of the time—this is not an undervaluation to make this point; it is genuine.

Why is this?

Is my work not to a suitable level? Of course it is.

It is because in that pitch, other people have a better relationship than I do with the decision-maker(s). Simple as that. This does not always mean it is personal. That relationship may help with true budgets, content or the direction the client is going in to give my competitors an unfair advantage when tendering. When I have the relationship in a presentation and I know my work is of high quality, I win 98 percent of the time. *Truthfully, it is even higher than this, but I did not want to appear arrogant.*

How do I know this?

A tender process normally consists of three to five companies that are asked to present to win a contract of works. All parties receive the same brief and budget. You are judged on your merits using the budget and interpretation of their vision to win. Completely fair. But it is not.

I have entered into pitches where a 'client of mine' has asked two other companies to tender to make the process 'seem fair' just so I can win it.

How do I know this? Because they have told me.

Why should I then be shocked if this happens to me? Exactly! I should not!

To think any aspect of life or business is truly fair is naive. In business and all other facets of life, it is who you know and how you know them, followed by your work quality in most industries that have nuances. The questions I give to every salesperson who works for me are 'How well do you know your clients?' and 'How can you get to know them better?' In the long term, this is the key to success!

As a small business, this is in your control. If you concentrate long enough and hard enough, even the hardest people can be won over. It just takes time. The fact that your business should be niche-targeted anyway, as mentioned in Lesson 9, should hold you in good stead.

BRINGING IT ALL TOGETHER

If you have reached this stage, congratulations! You have built something that has survived, thrived, and evolved into a success. Be proud. About 11 percent of businesses in the UK close every year, according to www.ons.gov.uk. So you are the exception, not the rule, at this point. Take a second to appreciate this.

For me, I always task myself with the next stage. This book has brought this to the forefront of my mind. Someone once said you very rarely have more than one successful business. Why would you ever leave it?

If I look back at how it started and the circumstances, why would I ever trade that in?

The next stage for each business owner is individual. Do you focus on growth? Sales? Streamlining? New territories? The options are endless.

For me, it has never been about greed. If I can give back to my staff and give them a piece of the business, they will forever be tied in and own something they have helped build. No person or business ever did it on their own, and this reward is what they deserve. They may not have had the ability to do what I did at the beginning, but they helped grow and develop the business as if they did. This is the next stage of my journey.

The experience so far has been far more rewarding personally, professionally and financially than I could have ever hoped. The hardest parts and lowest days make the appreciation for where we are as a company and where I am now far more rewarding.

I have learnt so much on my journey, and I hope that in sharing it, I will spare you some of the pain. At a minimum, at least you should have a better idea of what you are getting into. Here is a recap of what I discussed in this book:

1. Being a business owner is one of the hardest things you can do. But do not fret—you can do it!
2. There is no get-rich-quick scheme. You need a mixture of hard work, patience and a viable business idea.
3. Breaking it down into bite-sized chunks can make it more manageable and easier to succeed.
4. Make sure you have a viable business plan. This is the foundation for future success.
5. Not all decisions you make will be logical. Trust your gut instinct.
6. Get a mentor. Make sure you have someone to share experiences, ideas and feedback with.
7. Family have their place. But don't rely on them for anything more than support.

8. There is no right way to finance a business. Explore the options. Choose one that works best for you.

9. Make sure you know who your target market is. Make it niche.

10. Try to sell a service rather than a product. The upside and pitfalls are much better for a service offering.

11. A small business has numerous benefits. Make sure you work them to your advantage.

12. This could be the first day of the rest of your life. Be prepared. Be organised. Enjoy it.

13. Your first week is going to be exhausting. Make sure you appreciate everything you have learnt.

14. A CEO is the answer to all questions. The solver of all problems. The head of all departments. Be the expert.

15. Make sure the customer *loves* what you do!

16. Prepare for the first years of the business to be selfish and time-consuming. Find balance where you can.

17. Doing the easy things is not actually easy. You need to work at it every day.

18. Concentrate on the small wins. Eventually the big wins will take care of themselves.

19. Losing is a waste of everyone's time and effort. You do not have to like it!

20. Fight for every deal, no matter how lost it seems.

21. Setting up a company to make a difference or be the best will hold you in good stead. Do not do it for the money.

22. Principled decisions in the long run can define a business and its culture.

23. If you own the company, you are accountable for everything. Embrace this mindset.

24. Mistakes cost money. Do not keep making them.

25. Keep your fixed overheads as low as you can. They can be a drain on a business.
26. Do not pay for paper advertising—it is a waste of money.
27. Make sure you know what you are looking for in a team. They will define the culture.
28. Work ethic and talent are the two drivers of hiring success. Make sure you recruit well.
29. Managing people is one of the hardest parts of the job. Make sure you want to do it before growing your business.
30. Failure can be acceptable. Excuses are not. Make sure you can identify both.
31. A bad hire can cause far-reaching problems for a business both short- and long-term. Choose wisely.
32. If you are going to sack someone, do it properly.
33. When you finish a year, make sure you do an honest review. This is a perfect time to look at the business from afar and make changes.
34. Make sure you are assessing your success at all possible opportunities. Listen to external feedback from clients. It is invaluable.
35. Get awards—this is instant social and industrial reputation.
36. The CEO role will change as the company develops. Be willing to make that move.
37. Sales is a department that is black and white. Use this to your advantage.
38. You should be building a business for the future as well as the present. Make long-term relationships that can benefit the company in future years.
39. It is going to be a rollercoaster. Whether it is staff changes, market changes or unexpected surprises, everyday is a learning curve.

40. Dont underestimate the work that goes in behind the scene to win a deal. its not all about your product.

As I said in the introduction, if I had known how hard and difficult the next five years would be, I still would have done it again. Just tell me where to sign up.

I do not pretend to be perfect (I am far from it!) and will continue to make numerous mistakes on my business and personal journey. I do not doubt I have hundreds upon hundreds of lessons still to be learnt and unique and wonderful stories to experience. I embrace this anticipation.

With an open mind and a willingness to learn, I know I am not even close to the end of this company life cycle or my personal journey. I cannot wait to see what the outside world and the people at our company throw at me.

I look back and cannot believe what we have created. It is surreal and fills me with a sense of pride that bursts out of me when I tell people about it—a bit like those people that talk about their Tesla I mentioned!

There is no part of me that is not mentally stronger, wiser or more resilient as a result of starting a business. Very few people get to experience such an adventure. I am grateful that I am here every day.

I could not have done it without my team. I made them better, but they made me a better CEO. Our next stage is dedicated to them. Who will you dedicate your beginning to?

Good luck,

Chris

For further resources, please see:

www.chrisdale.com

ABOUT THE AUTHOR

CHRIS DALE is not a household name. And this is the point. He is also a self-made multi million-pound-turnover CEO of two multi-award-winning niche businesses...that you have never heard of. This is because this is what he set out to create. Over the past five years, he set out to document the journey of a small business owner. From director of a market-leading business, he took the leap into business ownership in five weeks, from scratch.